ISBN 978-1-332-03478-9
PIBN 10273186

This book is a reproduction of an important historical work. Forgotten Books uses state-of-the-art technology to digitally reconstruct the work, preserving the original format whilst repairing imperfections present in the aged copy. In rare cases, an imperfection in the original, such as a blemish or missing page, may be replicated in our edition. We do, however, repair the vast majority of imperfections successfully; any imperfections that remain are intentionally left to preserve the state of such historical works.

# 1 MONTH OF
# FREE
# READING

## at
## www.ForgottenBooks.com

By purchasing this book you are eligible for one month membership to ForgottenBooks.com, giving you unlimited access to our entire collection of over 700,000 titles via our web site and mobile apps.

To claim your free month visit:
www.forgottenbooks.com/free273186

English
Français
Deutsche
Italiano
Español
Português

# www.forgottenbooks.com

**Mythology** Photography **Fiction**
Fishing Christianity **Art** Cooking
Essays Buddhism Freemasonry
Medicine **Biology** Music **Ancient
Egypt** Evolution Carpentry Physics
Dance Geology **Mathematics** Fitness
Shakespeare **Folklore** Yoga Marketing
**Confidence** Immortality Biographies
Poetry **Psychology** Witchcraft
Electronics Chemistry History **Law**
Accounting **Philosophy** Anthropology
Alchemy Drama Quantum Mechanics
Atheism Sexual Health **Ancient History**
**Entrepreneurship** Languages Sport
Paleontology Needlework Islam
**Metaphysics** Investment Archaeology
Parenting Statistics Criminology
**Motivational**

# Sixteenth-Century Bristol

*(Originally published under the title of*
*"THE CORPORATION OF BRISTOL IN THE OLDEN TIME")*

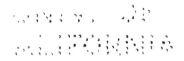

BY

## JOHN LATIMER

1908
BRISTOL
J. W. ARROWSMITH, 11 QUAY STREET
LONDON
SIMPKIN, MARSHALL, HAMILTON, KENT & COMPANY LIMITED

# PREFACE.

THE following papers on Bristol history during the reigns of Henry VIII. and his three successors are chiefly founded on extracts from the account books of the Corporation, ancient deeds and other documents, and the minutes of the Privy Council. They began to appear in the *Bristol Mercury* of December 27th, 1902, and were continued at weekly intervals during the following four months.

J. LATIMER.

*April*, 1903.

# PUBLISHER'S NOTE.
THE foregoing Preface and some alterations and additions to the original articles, included in a copy presented by Mr. LATIMER to the city, have been incorporated in this book by the kindness of the City Librarian, Mr. E. R. NORRIS MATHEWS.

# CONTENTS.

# Sixteenth-Century Bristol.

## CHAPTER I.

*Bristol in the early sixteenth century—Description of the town — Surrounded by religious houses — Numerous public holidays—Endowments, chantries and obits—Religious and secular pageants—St. Catherine's Eve—Shooting and wrestling competitions in the Marsh (Queen Square)—Play-actors and bear-keepers—Bear-baiting and bull-baiting—Feast of St. Nicholas; ceremony of the boy-bishop—Public executions—Christmas festivities.*

PERHAPS it may not be uninteresting to readers with some taste for local history to give a few facts from authentic records respecting the life and doings of Bristolians in the far-off days of Henry VIII. The most important of these records are the account books of the Corporation, which commence in 1531; but they can be supplemented and illustrated by various other contemporary documents, and some of the contrasts that can thus be made between the social customs of the sixteenth and of the twentieth centuries may prove at least amusing, if not instructive.

The transcendent circumstance which differentiates the Bristol which saw the accession of Henry from the city of to-day is the religious faith of the inhabitants. Roman Catholicism, at the former period, had reached the climax of its magnificence. It was the Church both of the State and of the people, and there was not a whisper of dissent, for nonconformity was punishable with a cruel death. The young King was a fervent devotee, and an amateur theologian, and his book against Luther gained for him from the Pope, in 1521, the proud title of Defender of the Faith. A very few years sufficed to work revolutionary changes, but it may be worth while to endeavour to form an idea of what was really the local situation at the date that has just been named.

The town—for it had not become a city—was extremely limited in area, and does not appear to have much increased in population during the previous two hundred years, having in the meanwhile been frightfully ravaged by the Black Death and the Plague. It may be broadly described as being bounded by Dolphin Street and Temple Street on the east, the course of the Froom along Broadmead to St. Augustine's Back on the north and west, and the town wall between Redcliff and Temple Gates on the south.

Around all this boundary line were institutions, independent of corporate jurisdiction. The Royal Castle, with its extensive fortified precincts, and the church and monastic buildings of the Black Friars, lay on the east. The Priory of St. James, and its adjoining farm lands, covered a vast space on the north. The Grey Friary, the Nunnery of St. Mary Magdalene, the Hospital of St. Bartholomew, the Carmelite Friary, the Hospital of the Gaunts, and the Abbey of St. Augustine, each enclosing wide areas around their respective churches and houses, entirely surrounded the north-western side of the borough, while the Hospital of St. John the Baptist and the Augustinian Friary, lying to the south, continued the circuit to Temple Fee, belonging to the military monks of

St. John, who repudiated the civic jurisdiction claimed by the Corporation. There was thus no room for suburbs outside the walls, even if there had been a desire for them ; but there is no evidence to show that the townsfolk felt any objection to the ecclesiastical circumvallation. Many of their wills attest rather their satisfaction at the multitude of their ghostly comforters. A few years later seven of the monkish churches around the city had been swept away, and half of two others was demolished ; but though there was a rush to get a share of the royal plunder, few additional dwellings were reared on the vacant sites until a much later date.

Another peculiarity arising from the then national faith was the remarkable number of public holidays. A chronicler of the fifteenth century observed that in the agricultural districts the aggregate number of holidays accounted for eight weeks in every year. The total can hardly have been so large in trading towns, but it was still very notable. Great church festivals, called Red Letter Days, were of frequent occurrence, when attendance at morning service was obligatory, and as business of all kinds was suspended for " a general procession " of the civic body, it is unlikely that much work was done in the afternoon. Many wealthy Bristolians, again, had bequeathed large sums for the establishment of what were called chantries in the parish churches, where, in addition to daily prayers for the founders' souls by the chaplain or chaplains supported by each endowment, a grand anniversary service, called an Obit, was held yearly, attracting a vast attendance of all classes.

In 1548, when these endowments were seized for the profit of the Crown, an inquiry was held in Bristol by the

Royal Commissioners to ascertain the value of the local estates.   The amount reported by them was probably grossly underestimated, for one of the inquisitors, a notorious gambler (afterwards hanged) named Partridge, forestalled all would-be purchasers by obtaining from his employers, the Government, a grant of the entire property *en bloc;* while a congenial colleague, Sir William Sharington, master of the Bristol Mint, who confessed in the following year to having committed enormous frauds in coining base money, lent Partridge the purchase money, and took fully one-half of the spoil as his own reward. Even if the value of the estates were justly rendered, the total, £360 per annum, was equivalent to ten times that amount in modern currency.   The chantries of Evrard le French and William Canynges in St. Nicholas and Redcliff Churches were returned as of the yearly value of over £33 each, and supported four priests, who had no other duties to perform.   A rich merchant, named Knapp, not only founded a chantry with two priests, but built a special chapel for it, dedicated to St. John, on the Welsh Back, the site of which is now* a little playground.   About twenty other chantries had at least one priest each, independent of the parish incumbents, and if we add about thirty friars, who held daily services in their four churches, but were all paid for taking part in " general processions," the number of available clergymen in the town four hundred years ago, exclusive of the numerous monks in two large monasteries, must have far exceeded the staff of the ancient parishes in the present day.

It remains to be seen how these institutions affected public holidays.   An anniversary Obit took place on the average about once in three weeks all the year round, and

* 1902.  The playground has since been done away with.

potent means for securing the attendance of the townsfolk had been taken by the chantry founders. As a fair example of the general custom to secure the presence of the Mayor and Corporation in full state, the proctors of Hallewey's Chantry in All Saints' Church were directed to pay 6s. 8d. to the Mayor, 3s. 4d. to each of the Sheriffs, 1s. to the Town Clerk, 4d. to the Swordbearer, and 3d. each to the four civic sergeants, while, to allure the working classes, a silver penny was given to each of six hundred persons—about one-fifth of the adult population when the chantry was established, and when the daily wage of an unskilled labourer did not exceed the amount of the dole. It is not surprising that work came to a standstill when an attractive street spectacle was backed by the prospect of pecuniary profit.

Besides the Obits, there were various occasional pageants, some religious, some secular. About Whitsuntide the Guilds of Weavers and Cordwainers yearly went in pompous array to the Chapel of St. Anne-in-the-Wood, near Brislington, a spot greatly frequented by pilgrims, and more than once visited by Royalty, to place before the altar two gigantic candles, alleged by William of Worcester to have been of the somewhat incredible length of eighty feet each, and to have cost no less than £5— equal to the quarterly " wages " of the Mayor. A few weeks before midsummer brought round the feast of Corpus Christi, one of the greatest holidays of the year. The members of every guild—and practically every Bristolian belonged to a guild—assembled with music, flags and banners to join in a splendid ecclesiastical procession through the streets, where the houses were decorated with tapestry, brilliant cloth, and garlands of flowers, and the afternoon was spent in the performance in the open air of miracle plays, in which every craft claimed its special part, to the enjoyment of the whole community. The excitement caused by this festival can have scarcely subsided before the inhabitants were called upon to participate in the corporate parade, called the "Setting of the Watch" on Midsummer Eve.

In imitation of a similar ceremony in London, which cost an enormous sum yearly, the members of the chief trade companies—who emulated each other in the display of gay dresses, banners, burning " cressets " and torches, and in the supply of minstrels and musical instruments— marched in procession through the streets, the proceedings terminating in morris dancing and various games, in which the populace participated. The Corporation left the chief expenditure of the day to be defrayed by the guilds, but provided 114 gallons of wine, presumably for the subsequent suppers of the companies—the weavers and tuckers receiving ten gallons each, whilst the remainder was distributed amongst the other twenty-six fraternities. When the streets were muddy, and they were rarely otherwise, the city treasurer also paid the cost of covering them with twenty or thirty tons of sand.

Another civic outlay of the day is somewhat puzzling. It would appear that the procession ended and the sports began upon Bristol Bridge, and to that spot a great quantity of nettles, cut down in the Marsh (Queen Square), were invariably transported beforehand at the corporate charge. The only plausible conjecture that can be suggested to explain this outlay is that the stinging plants were provided for a rough-and-tumble scuffle. Another "Setting of the Watch," of a precisely similar character (nettles included), took place on St. Peter's Day in August.

The eve of St. Catherine, in November, was the most

notable festival of the weavers, then the leading and most numerous local handicraft. According to the Mayor's Kalendar, written about 1490, the Mayor and members of the Corporation, after having been entertained in the Weavers' Hall, near Temple Church, on spiced cake, bread and wine, " the cups merrily filled about the house," returned to their homes, " ready to receive at their doors St. Katherine's players, making them to drink at their doors, and rewarding them for their plays," which must thus have been performed in the open streets. A grand procession through all the thoroughfares took place on the following morning.

The Corporation also made provision for various out-door sports. Extensive butts were maintained in the Marsh for the practice of archery, which was then obliga-tory on all capable of bearing arms, and the place was largely resorted to by bowmen on Sunday afternoons in the summer months. In July a day was set apart for wrestling matches in the Marsh, and another and more popular competition of the same sort, between townsmen and countrymen took place at Lawrencetide, in August, at Lawrence Hill, a prize of 6s. 8d. being given out of the city purse on each occasion. As the second display required the corporate body to march a mile into the country, a " modest quencher" became, of course, indispensable, and in 1532 the city fathers disposed of six and a half gallons of wine, costing 5s. 5d. ; " more for bread, 1d., pears 2s. 4d." The bill for wine and fruit slightly varied in subsequent years, but the penny for bread was a fixed quantity, whatever might be the consumption of liquor. In 1543 there was a slight hitch in the arrangements, explained in the accounts as follows :—

" Paid  the wrestlers on  both sides, 4s.   The  old
custom was 6s. 8d., but for because the country side
brought not a goose according to the old custom, therefore was paid but 4s.   Spent  upon  them  at Laffords
Gate [to smooth matters over ?], 4d."

Soon  after this wrestling competition  the Worshipful
Mayor and his brethren suspended business at the Tolzey,
and gave themselves a holiday in order to enjoy the cheer-
ful sport of fishing in the Froom, in the presence of crowds
of spectators.   As sometimes as much as 4s. were paid " to
the men that went into the water," a large staff must have
been employed to drag the nets.   The catch must also have
been generally good, for on one occasion the Mayor was
paid 10s. " because he did not go a-fishing."

Other causes of distraction from work came from outside the city in the shape of travelling companies of play-
actors and bear-keepers.   The King and several noblemen
maintained these parties of strangers, who were allowed to
travel about the country when they were not required at
Court, and were always welcome.   In 1532 the Corporation
gave 10s. to the players of Lord Lisle and 6s. 6d. to those
of the Duke of Richmond, the King's illegitimate son,
whom  Henry once contemplated to proclaim heir to the
throne.   In the same year, from 3s. 4d. to 5s. each were
bestowed on the bear-wards of the Duke of Suffolk, Lord
Westmoreland, and the Duke of Richmond.   Bear-baiting
and bull-baiting were two of the most favourite " sports "
of the age, and as, unlike the drama, they could be
witnessed free of expense, every exhibition attracted
thousands of working men.

The civic ceremony which seems the most extraordinary
to modern ideas was that which took place on December

6th, the feast of St. Nicholas. At this festival a boy, doubtless one of the servitors of the parish priests, was solemnly instituted as a bishop, and having been clothed in episcopal vestments, delivered a sermon in St. Nicholas' Church, before the Mayor and Common Council, on whom he gravely pronounced his blessing. And then, says the Mayor's Kalendar, the spelling of which we modernise :—

"After dinner, the said Mayor, Sheriff, and their brethren to assemble at the Mayor's compter, there waiting the bishop's coming, playing the meanwhiles at dice ; the town clerk to find them dice, and to have one penny of every raffle ; and when the bishop is come thither, his chapel there to sing, and the bishop to give them his blessing ; and then he and all his chapel to be served there with bread and wine. And so depart the Mayor, Sheriff, and their brethren to hear the bishop's evensong at St. Nicholas' Church."

The ceremony of the boy bishop was of ancient date, and was practised in all parts of the kingdom. In 1299 Edward I. rewarded one of these mock prelates at Newcastle with a sum now equivalent to £40. But conceive the Bristol Council of our day solemnly assembled to receive a madrigal boy befigged as a bishop, whiling away their time with the dice box which the Town Clerk—on the look-out for his fee—had at hand for the Lord Mayor, and making four processions through the crowded streets to and from sham services at St. Nicholas !

It is perhaps hardly fair to include public executions in the list of holidays, and yet they unquestionably filled the streets with non-workers. They occurred once (and sometimes twice) every year as a certain issue of the sessions, and there was always a small payment for

" carrying the ladder to and from St. Michael's Hill."
There being no carts in Bristol, the unhappy convicts had
to make their long journey from Newgate to Cotham on
foot, and were swung off the ladder by the hangman.

Finally, during Christmas week, the lord of misrule
was in full supremacy, and holiday keeping generally
extended from Christmas Eve to Twelfth Night. A day or
two before the festivities the Mayor, for the sake of public
order, made public proclamation that no inhabitant,
gentle or simple, should go about mumming with masked
faces at night after the tolling of the curfew bell unless he
carried a torch, lantern, candle, or sconce, and that no one
should wear weapons by night or by day, on pain of fine
or imprisonment. In a season of universal license it may
be questioned whether much heed was paid to the regula-
tions. It was the season of unlimited guzzling, the city
magnates setting the example. By an ordinance of the
Common Council in 1472, the Mayor's Christmas drinking
was fixed to take place on St. Stephen's Day (December
26), the Sheriff's drinking on St. John's Day (December 27),
the senior Bailiff's drinking on Innocents' Day (December
28), and that of the junior Bailiff on New Year's Day.
" And on Twelfth Day to go to the Christmas drinking of
the Abbot of St. Augustine as of old custom, if it be prayed
by the Abbot and Convent."

# CHAPTER II.

ON a cursory examination of the corporate account books in the middle of Henry VIII.'s reign, the income and expenditure of the civic body appear to be marvellously insignificant as compared with the importance and reputation of the port and borough. In the year ending Michaelmas, 1536, for example, the total receipts of the Chamberlain (Treasurer) are stated to have been £186 8s. 11½d., whilst his outlay was no more than £161 10s. 1d. Further examination, however, reveals the fact that this official was the recipient of little more than the waifs and strays of the corporate revenue, and that the chief financial business was in the hands of the Sheriffs, whose accounts have not been preserved in the Council House. The true state of affairs is revealed in an elaborate document addressed to the all powerful minister, Cardinal

Wolsey, by William Dale, one of the Sheriffs elected in 1518, complaining of the manner in which he and his colleague, like all previous Sheriffs, had been victimised by the Common Council. According to the detailed figures which he set forth (which must be multiplied by twelve to represent the currency of modern days), the shrieval income, including £60 received from the Chamber, was £232 10s. 8d.

On the other hand, the Sheriffs were required to pay the fee-farm of the town, yearly due to the Crown, which with subsidiary expenses amounted to £172 ; to furnish the Mayor with his " pension " of £20 ; to provide his worship with a splendid robe of scarlet and fur, wine, minstrels, and many other items, costing altogether £37 ; to disburse all the charges for watches, wrestlings, bear-baitings, and Christmas drinkings referred to in the previous chapter, which, with other like matters, involved an outlay of over £46 ; to pay the salaries of the Recorder, Town Clerk, Town Steward, Town Attorney, Priest of St. George's Chapel, porters of the town gates, and minor corporate officials, and to bedeck the whole of them with robes, at a total outlay of over £100 ; to defray the cost of the Sessions, £12 ; to pay the wages of the members of Parliament for the city when at Westminster, 2s. per day each ; to keep in order St. Nicholas' clock ; to give doles to the four orders of Friars, &c. ; the aggregate outlay amounting to over £378. Mr. Dale and his companion were thus out of pocket £146, exclusive of £240 alleged to be " both Sheriffs' expenses and costs of household, and the apparel of them and their wives."

The Common Council were highly indignant at these revelations, and warmly protested that the expenditure of the Sheriffs was in accordance with ancient custom, and that the charges, alleged to be partly exaggerated and partly due to "high and prodigal minds," might well be borne by prosperous men in consideration of the worshipful dignity conferred upon them. The Cardinal, nevertheless, commanded a reform of the system ; and in 1519 the Corporation, doubtless much against its will, made new arrangements. The allowance of £60 to the Sheriffs was discontinued ; but the dues derived from shipping entering the port, then amounting to nearly £83, were thenceforth to be received by the Sheriffs, together with the tolls collected at the town gates, £57. Their customary income derived from the great St. James's Fair, £23 ; from law fines and forfeitures, £30 ; and £12, the profits of the gaol (for, strange to say, the gaol was a profitable institution) were to be retained, and a few trifling items raised the shrieval income to £215. As regarded expenditure, the Sheriffs were relieved from the expense of the Mayor's "pension" and robes, and from the wages (but not from the robes) of the Recorder and city officers, whilst a few charges for wrestlings, drinkings, &c., were also transferred to the Chamber, their total expenditure being thus cut down to £273, being still an excess over income of £58. Subsequent Sheriffs must nevertheless have been grateful to Mr. Dale and the Cardinal.

The custom of demanding toll at the town gates on goods entering or leaving a fortified borough was originally established for the purpose of maintaining the walls, and was probably universal in the Middle Ages. Even to the present day the Corporation of Newcastle* derives a great yearly income from this source, and the proceeds of the octroi at Paris meet the ordinary outlay of the municipality. The system, however, was very unpopular in

* The collection of the Thorough Toll, Newcastle-on-Tyne, will cease on August 5th, 1910.

Bristol, and the complaints of the inhabitants eventually culminated in scenes of violence. In 1546 a happy thought suggested itself to some worthy citizen, and was received with general applause. As need hardly be stated, the then recent suppression of the monasteries had led to the seizure by the Crown of an almost fabulous amount of wealth in the shape of gold and silver plate, many cart-loads of such treasure having been secured at Canterbury, Durham and York, and vast quantities in the wealthier abbeys. In the year just named the Government had already turned a covetous eye on the chantries in the cathedrals and parish churches, which with many " free chapels " were upwards of 2,300 in number, and there was ample reason for suspecting that the churches themselves —which were richly stored with valuables in the shape of processional crosses, monstrances, incense boxes, thuribles, and eucharistic vessels—would not long escape spoliation.

Now the Corporation had succeeded in obtaining from the King in 1540 an extensive grant of the estates of the dissolved religious houses, and a further grant in 1544 of properties in Bristol to be referred to presently, but had been forced to borrow the purchase moneys, £1,790, and was in painful financial straits. The pro-pounder of the brilliant idea just referred to suggested that the parochial vestries should offer the Corporation a quantity of plate sufficient to pay off a large portion of its liabilities, on condition of its surrendering its rights to levy tolls. The proposal having been approved by fourteen out of the seventeen city parishes, and eagerly accepted by the Common Council, the accounts of the Sheriffs for the previous ten years were examined to ascertain the amount received at the gates, and also the sum collected in the shape of dues on victuals and grain of all kinds, wool, yarn and flannel brought to the quays by ships.    In the result, a net sum of £44 per annum was settled upon as adequate compensation to be paid by the Council to the Sheriffs for the abolition of the tolls and dues.    The fourteen vestries thereupon produced plate to the value of £523 10s. 8d., taking security from the Corporation to be borne harmless in case the treasure should be thereafter claimed by the Crown.

By the aid of this handsome gift the civic body over-came its pecuniary embarrassments, and entered into full possession of the estates of Gaunt's Hospital (save the rich manor of Pawlett, in Somerset), the Bristol houses of the Grey and Carmelite Friars, the manor of Hamp, formerly belonging to Athelney Abbey, and a slice of land, previously the property of the Magdalene Nunnery, on St. Michael's Hill, for all which the Crown had received £1,000, and also of the Bristol properties still to be described.    (The country estates of Gaunt's Hospital were sold in 1836 for nearly £60,000.    Colston Hall and the property in the rear, including the Red Lodge, represent the site of the Carmelite Friary.)    On June 14th, 1546, a formal agreement was drawn up between the Corporation and " the discreet and loving burgesses," whereby it was declared that, after due deliberation of the disquietness created by the tolls, the perjuries and blasphemies caused by them, and the evil slanders against the city thereby arising, and in further consideration of the future good of the city and of those resorting to it, all the gates should be thenceforth freed from all manner of tolls, and that no shipping dues should be levied on the goods and wares mentioned above.    The relief from an oppressive burden was proclaimed at the High Cross amidst general re-joicing.

Not the slightest allusion is to be found in the corporate account books to the purchases from the Crown or to the contributions of the parishes. The transactions were doubtless dealt with in a separate volume, since lost. Certain " church plate," probably from St. Mark's Church (Mayor's Chapel) was carried to the Council House, in order to be " sent to London," and 16d. was spent " for beer, ale and wine," drank when the plate was counted and packed into baskets for the carrier. But no time was lost in turning the acquired property to account. The Friary buildings were at once converted into quarries. " Paid two men for choosing out of the Friars certain paving stones to pave withal, 2s. 6d." Hundreds of sledge loads of stone, including chimney pieces and other ornamental work were afterwards drawn from thence for building purposes. As the gross rents of the monastic estates amounted to £266 in 1548, when they make their first appearance in the audit book, it is clear that the purchase produced an enormous return from the outset.

The second royal grant to the Corporation was of much less value than the first, but it definitely settled a controversy that had been a chronic trouble for many generations. Early in the twelfth century, Robert Fitzroy, Earl of Gloucester, lord of the great manor of Bedminster, which then extended to Bristol Bridge, granted to the Order of Templars a portion of the borough of Redcliff, which severed portion was thenceforth known as Temple Fee. On the ruthless destruction of the Templars in the reign of Edward II. this Fee was part of the estate which the King conferred on the knights of St. John of Jerusalem, and formed part of their preceptory of Temple Combe. The new owners, like their predecessors, were empowered to hold their own courts, to execute felons, and to exercise all other feudal privileges in their domains, independent of the ordinary authorities. When Redcliff became incorporated with Bristol, the attempts of the Corporation to extend their jurisdiction over Temple Fee, which seems to have become a refuge for outlaws, was strongly resisted by order of the non-resident knights, and civic officials pursuing malefactors appear to have frequently returned with empty hands and broken heads. In 1532, when the contest for jurisdiction was in one of its acute stages, a member of the Order, styled " the Knight of Rodys " (Rhodes) in the corporate accounts, paid a visit to Bristol to discuss the matter, and was entertained by the city with two gallons of wine and a quantity of sweetmeats, without anything being gained by the expenditure.

No settlement being effected, the respective parties appealed to the King, the Prior of St. John, who had a seat in the House of Lords, alleging that Temple Street, as part of the Fee, enjoyed liberty of sanctuary for felons and murderers, and that his tenants there had a right to buy and sell though not burgesses of Bristol, claiming also to hold courts, and to have the return and execution of writs, all which privileges were denied by the Corporation. The King referred the dispute to two of the superior judges, who, after hearing evidence, adjudged in 1535 that the civic officers had a right to arrest felons in the Fee and to execute writs, but postponed their decision on other points. Troubles with the military monks came to a summary end in 1541, when their possessions were confiscated. In 1544 the Corporation petitioned the King for a grant of the lands, quit-rents, &c., of the Fee, and the advowson of Temple Church, estimating the yearly value at £14 7s. 11d. They also prayed to be granted the estate in Bristol, then lately belonging to Viscount Lisle,* but fallen into the King's hands, the annual value being estimated at £57 8s. 3d. His Majesty acceded to the request, and granted both the estates in consideration of a payment of £789 17s. 10d. The above estimates of value are shown to have been pretty accurate by the civic audit book for 1548, in which the properties make their first appearance. The rents had produced £94, reduced to about £68 by outlay for repairs.

The corporate estates were not secured by a simple payment of the King's demands for their concession. The civil government of the country, after the fall of Wolsey, fell into the hands of Thomas Cromwell, whose insatiable rapacity was phenomenal even in his own time. The astonishing results are to be read in the State Papers of the reign. It came to be universally understood that any claim, however just, and any petition, however reasonable, addressed to the despotic monarch was doomed to certain rejection unless favoured by the Minister, and that such favour was hopeless unless purchased by a bribe. A golden stream flowing from all ranks accordingly set in, and yearly increased. Even

* Derivation of the civic estate known as "Lord Lisle's Lands."

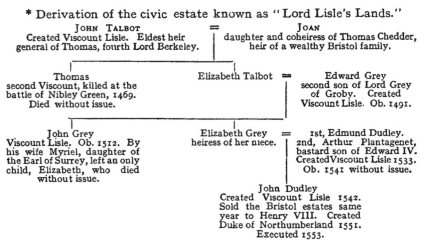

JOHN TALBOT
Created Viscount Lisle. Eldest heir general of Thomas, fourth Lord Berkeley.

= 

JOAN
daughter and coheiress of Thomas Chedder, heir of a wealthy Bristol family.

Thomas
second Viscount, killed at the battle of Nibley Green, 1469. Died without issue.

Elizabeth Talbot =

Edward Grey
second son of Lord Grey of Groby. Created Viscount Lisle. Ob. 1491.

John Grey
Viscount Lisle. Ob. 1512. By his wife Myriel, daughter of the Earl of Surrey, left an only child, Elizabeth, who died without issue.

Elizabeth Grey
heiress of her niece.

=

1st, Edmund Dudley. 2nd, Arthur Plantagenet, bastard son of Edward IV. Created Viscount Lisle 1533. Ob. 1541 without issue.

John Dudley
Created Viscount Lisle 1542. Sold the Bristol estates same year to Henry VIII. Created Duke of Northumberland 1551. Executed 1553.

before the monasteries were threatened, abbots and priors vied with each other in showering gratifications on the dreaded Secretary. When they fell, and the Court was besieged by innumerable suitors for a share in the gigantic spoil, the flood of money that poured into the Vicar-General's coffers must have astounded even himself. (A characteristic example of his unscrupulousness occurred shortly before his fall. In August, 1539, Gwylliams, the last abbot of St. Augustine's, transmitted him a bribe of £100 to secure the Royal confirmation to that office, which he was forced to surrender only four months later.) The Corporation of Bristol took a just measure of Cromwell's character at an early date. In 1533, the office of Recorder falling vacant, it was conferred upon the Secretary as a sinecure, bringing in £20 a year, and securing his countenance, which was the one thing needful. It may be safely assumed that a larger gratification had to be offered to him when the negotiation was opened for the Gaunt estates, but the records have disappeared. The Royal grant had passed the Great Seal only a few weeks when Cromwell, having served his master's purposes, met with the customary fate of Tudor instruments. The following entries occur in the civic account book for 1540 :—

" Paid to the Lord Privy Seal by the hands of Mr. Davy Broke, Recorder, £20." [Note by the Auditors] " Forasmuch the £20 charged paid to the Lord Essex, late Recorder, for his fee due to him at the Feast of the Nativity, 1540, which accustomally was used to be then paid at won [*sic*] time, and for that this said Lord of Essex was beheaded before the said feast in the said year, we the Auditors find that the £20 ought not to be allowed in this account."

How this little difficulty was settled does not appear.

The fall of Cromwell was followed by the rise of
another ignoble and greedy tool of despotism, Edward,
brother of Queen Jane Seymour, created Earl of Hertford
and Duke of Somerset, who afterwards usurped the place
of Lord Protector. Seymour had Bristol blood in his
veins, and the Corporation, with its usual predilection for
a powerful friend at Court, invented the office of Lord
High Steward, endowed it with a yearly fee of £4, and
presented it to the rising luminary. Soon after the death
of Henry VIII., Somerset and his myrmidons laid hands
on the chantries in the manner narrated in the previous
chapter, and the Protector paid a visit to Bristol to watch
local operations. His inquisitorial commissions reached
the city about the same time, and were profusely entertained by the Corporation, which, with a sharp eye for
contingencies, presented the Lord High Steward with
his " fee," accompanied by two butts of wine, and paid
the charges of his retinue. The results proved highly
satisfactory. The chantries with all their estates and
effects were, of course, entirely swallowed up. The
Merchant Venturers' Chapel of St. Clement, the Weavers'
Chapel of St. Catherine, the Tailors' Chapel of St. John,
and Knapp's Chapel on the Back were suppressed, and
their contents confiscated. Services at the Chapel of
St. George in the Guildhall were stopped, and the image
of the patron saint was torn down. The Chapel of the
Three Kings of Cologne at Christmas Steps and Trinity
Chapel in the Old Market, both attached to almshouses, of
which the Corporation were trustees, were not included
in the sale of the chantry estates. The Commissioners,
however, decreed that they were the property of the
Crown, and ordered the confiscation of so much of each
of the hospital estates as was equivalent in yearly value

to the stipend of each of the dispossessed chaplains (about £6). This decision appears to have been long over-looked. But it was discovered in 1577 by two legal sharpers, who forthwith procured a grant of the two chapels and the reserved lands from Queen Elizabeth. The grantees then came down upon the Corporation, who were compelled to submit to their terms, and who paid them £66 13s. 4d. for a transfer of the Queen's con-veyance.

The Chapel of St. Mary on Bristol Bridge, with the adjoining dwelling of the priest, was bestowed upon the corporate body, though the estates of the fabric went with the rest of the chantries. The transaction is re-corded in the audit book :—

Paid to the King for the purchase of the site, with
    the Priest's Chamber, and the lead, with all
    the appurtenances belonging to the same ..  £40
More to the King for the bells and all the vest-
    ments and implements    ..  ..  ..  ..  £11

There were, however, large incidental expenses. Several journeys had to be made to London to get the grant passed in due form. The Lord Chancellor had to be paid for the patent, the Lord Privy Seal had to be feed for the signet, and gratuities had to be offered to Court underlings, scribes, and attorneys, the total expenditure being thereby raised to nearly £88. But, on the other hand, the proctors and auditors of the chapel paid over funds in hand (of which, it may be safely suspected, the royal agents had been kept in the dark) amounting in round figures to £55 ; the bells and implements sold for £11 ; and one, Mrs. Compton, paid £6 13s. 4d. " for the consideration that Sir Thomas, her kinsman, might be admitted to the same service "—that is, be appointed chaplain, which he possibly was for life. The actual outlay by the Corporation was thus reduced to a few pounds. The chapel extended right across the bridge, being erected over an archway similar to that of St. John's Church in Broad Street.

In 1553 another gang of spoliators was nominated by the Government to confiscate the plate of all the churches in the kingdom, and Bristolians had good reason to congratulate themselves on their proceedings in 1546. With the exception of two small chalices in the Cathedral, and one in each of the parish churches, which were ordered " safely and surely to be kept for the King's Majesty's use," every precious article was carried off, together with most of the parochial bells. (The Cathedral was deprived of five great bells and nearly 130 tons of lead roofing.) The returns as to the quantity of plate actually seized have perished, but some conception of the total may be arrived at by recorded facts relating to St. Nicholas' Church. When the parochial gifts were made to procure the freedom of the gates this church possessed 694 ounces of silver ornaments, and the vestry contributed £46 15s., which, at 5s. 6d. per ounce, the current value of silver bullion, would represent 170 ounces. The Commissioners therefore swept off the remaining 524 ounces, less one chalice of 15 ounces, left to the parish. As regards All Saints' Church, a document is in existence proving that 420 ounces were taken thence to the Bristol Mint. These were probably the two wealthiest parishes in the city; but even the little parish of St. Leonard was despoiled of 222 ounces, and it may be fairly assumed that the aggregate spoil from the Cathedral and the seventeen parochial churches must have reached about 5,000 ounces of silver, to say nothing of the value of the lead and bells. The plate was probably removed to the local mint and converted into base money, the shillings coined by Sharington being intrinsically worth about threepence.

# CHAPTER III.

*Population of Bristol in the sixteenth century—Police and sanitary arrangements of the city—Prevalence of mendicants—Use of hops in ale prohibited ; thatch-roofing forbidden—Erection of houses by the Corporation on Bristol Bridge.*

To modern readers the most interesting fact preserved in the State papers in relation to the local chantries is the numbering of the inhabitants of Bristol, which they luckily record. The Royal mandate to the Chantry Commissioners required the churchwardens not only to produce a detailed account of the yearly proceeds of each chantry estate, but also to return the number of inhabitants dwelling in each parish, and this census accordingly stands at the head of each parochial report. Whatever may have been the knavery of the Commissioners in underestimating, for the benefit of two of themselves, the value of the confiscated property, neither the visitors nor the local authorities had any inducement to misrepresent the actual population of a city. In a few parishes the numbering seems to have been made with scrupulous exactness. In others the round figures show that the churchwardens were content to offer an approximate estimate of " the houseling people" living within their respective boundaries; but it is unlikely that any of the returns were intentionally magnified or diminished, for no purpose could be served by falsification. The following are the figures :—

24

| | | |
|---|---|--:|
| Parish of St. Werburgh | .. .. .. .. | 160 |
| ,, St. James | .. .. .. .. .. | 520 |
| ,, St. Thomas | .. .. .. .. .. | 600 |
| ,, St. Philip | .. .. .. .. .. | 514 |
| ,, St. John | .. .. .. .. .. | 227 |
| ,, St. Nicholas | .. .. .. .. .. | 800 |
| ,, St. Peter | .. .. .. .. .. | 400 |
| ,, Christ Church | .. .. .. .. | 326 |
| ,, St. Stephen | .. .. .. .. .. | 461 |
| ,, St. Mary Redcliff | .. .. .. .. | 600 |
| ,, All Saints | .. .. .. .. .. | 180 |
| ,, Temple | .. .. .. .. .. .. | 480 |
| ,, St. Ewen | .. .. .. .. .. | 56 |
| ,, St. Leonard | .. .. .. .. .. | 120 |
| ,, St. Michael | .. .. .. .. .. | 252 |
| ,, St. Mary-le-port | .. .. .. .. | 180 |

5876

As there were no chantries in St. Augustine-the-Less, which had been a dependency of the neighbouring abbey, a census of that parish does not appear. The number of inhabitants, however, must have been inconsiderable, for with the exception of a fringe of dwellings at and near St. Augustine's Back, College Green, Frog Lane, and Limekiln Road, the district was divided into grass land and garden ground. Thus the total population of the city apparently did not much exceed 6,000. Similar returns for the city of Gloucester show an aggregate population of 3,159.

One seeks in vain for definite information as to the police and sanitary arrangements that were in force at the date of the above census. In 1508 the Corporation passed an ordinance declaring that the mayor, two aldermen, and the forty " men " (common councillors) were entitled to

levy dues " on the goods of the townsmen, as well on rents
as on merchandise " ; but this power seems to have been
exercised only on great emergencies, and, if the audit books
may be trusted, local rates in the modern sense were unknown.    The paving of the chief thoroughfares was compulsory on the owners of the frontages, each maintaining
the surface of the street as far as the central gutter.    The
lighting of the streets at night was never dreamt of.    Such
scavenging as was thought indispensable was long undertaken by a single individual, who sought his remuneration
from the goodwill of the householders ;  but in 1543 the
Common Council resolved to pay this public servant 1s. 6d.
per week, or 20s. per quarter, and as the luckless " raker "
could not live on this stipend and continued his perquisi-
tions, he was afterwards voted 12s. a year extra " because
he shall take no toll."    In 1557 the Council increased his
salary to £12 per annum, but relief from this charge was
immediately secured by ordering a " collection " to be
made from the citizens.    It is not stated on what basis the
money was levied, but the whole outlay was brought in,
and the only corporate disbursement was twopence weekly
for keeping the front of the Council House and Guildhall
in decent order.    Even a parsimonious trader could hardly
have grumbled at having to contribute some small fraction
of a penny towards raising 4s. 6d. a week.    About the
same date the civic body laid out 3s. 8d. for a lantern to
hang at Froom Gate, and there is also mention of a lantern
at the High Cross, but no payment occurs for candles,
except occasionally on the Midsummer Watch night, when
sixpence might be laid out for " tapers " at the Cross.

Mendicants becoming increasingly troublesome, a new
official, styled the master of the beggars, was appointed in
1532, and provided with a yearly coat and the modest

salary of 3s. 4d. per quarter, subsequently raised to 5s., from which one must infer that he was employed rather for occasional show than for daily use. Mendicity, indeed, was not merely tolerated before the invention of poor rates, but actually patronised by the Corporation. The following items occur in the audit book under March, 1571 :—

> " Paid for graving a mould of the town's arms to cast in tin for 40 badges, to set upon 20 poor people to go into Somerset to seek relief, 2s. ; 7 lbs. tin to cast them, 4s. 8d. ; casting and making holes whereby they might be sewed upon their backs and breasts, 2s. 6d. ; thread, 1d."

Finally, the provisions for the suppression of crime and for the preservation of good order were ludicrously feeble. The Corporation maintained a staff of four sergeants, remunerated by fees. But these officers, when not in attendance upon the magistrates, as they were expected to be daily, were largely employed in the legal business arising out of civil actions in the Mayor's and Sheriffs' Courts, and naturally shirked all duties that offered no prospect of remuneration. Parish constables, again, were selected yearly—one half at the Midsummer Watch, and the others on St. Peter's Day—from the able-bodied residents of each ward ; but they rarely undertook active service except when specially summoned to quell disturbances, and casual brawls were left to settle them-selves. When a malefactor was not caught in the act, or left no traces of his identity, he had evidently little to fear in the shape of detection and retribution. One or two corporate ordinances presumably intended to promote the health and safety of the public may be briefly noted.

There is a current legend that the hop plant came into

England with the Reformation. But it was used by
Bristol brewers in the reign of Henry VII., to the discontent of the Common Council, who issued an edict in 1505,
forbidding hops to be put into ale except in the months of
June, July, and August, on pain of a penalty of 40s. And
apparently to detect infringements of this order, an " ale
conner " was appointed in 1519, who was ordered to go
boldly into every brewer's premises, to taste his ale, and if
it was found unwholesome, to forbid its sale. A few years
later this officer was deemed so useful that two " conners "
were appointed, with a joint yearly salary of £1 6s. 8d.

It was not until 1574 that an ordinance was enacted
forbidding the use of thatch for roofing houses and other
buildings in the city.

Soon after the Corporation had obtained the Royal
grant of the chapel on Bristol Bridge, it undertook a work
of some importance—the construction of two houses on the
same thoroughfare of a character far surpassing the
customary style of tradesmen's dwellings, which rarely
exceeded two stories in height. The project seems to
have been instigated by the receipt of a legacy of £100,
bequeathed for public purposes by one Thomas Hart, and
by the payment of one-half of a similar bequest of £40 left
by Thomas Silk. Moved by a somewhat cool appeal for
further assistance to carry out the design, Alderman
Thomas White, of London, a member of a Bristol family
remarkable for its liberal benefactions to the city, generously
presented another £100. With these funds in hand, the
Common Council, in 1548, gave orders for beginning the
work, which was executed by workmen paid weekly by the
Chamberlain. As the houses were to be chiefly of wood,
a carpenter was brought down from London as super-
intendent, and was paid one shilling per day, the local

workmen receiving eightpence, and the labourers fivepence per head. The first order for timber brought in seventeen large trees, and many more were required subsequently. The chimneys and fireplaces were of brick, which appears to have been imported, and was costly, two parcels costing £38. The bricklayer was paid one shilling per day. Some old glass was made available, and 258 feet of new glass cost the high price of sixpence per foot. Two of the Friaries were pillaged for some ornamental stonework. Probably owing to the workmen being left much to their own devices, the building operations extended over eighty-six weeks, and the total expenditure was no less than £495 13s. 9d., an extraordinary sum for that period. The houses were let for £6 13s. 4d. each in 1551, in which year the Corporation, which had just rebuilt the Tolzey in Corn Street as a Council House, set about the erection of a block of warehouses in the " Old Jewry," the locality inhabited by the Bristol Jews previous to their expulsion from England in 1290, and now represented by part of the buildings standing between Bell Lane and Quay Street. The outlay on this undertaking was £470. The cost of the new Tolzey or Council House cannot be ascertained.

# CHAPTER IV.

*Bristol and feudalism—Interference of Anne Boleyn in
Bristol affairs—Visit of Anne and Henry VIII. to
Thornbury—Suppression of St. John's Hospital;
unsuccessful attempt by Corporation to obtain possession
—Trouble with Lord President of Welsh Marches;
attempts to levy tribute from Bristol; his pretensions
finally put an end to — Seizure of Bristol corn by
Mayor of Gloucester—Persecution of Protestants in
Bristol—Accession of Elizabeth—Bristol trained bands
reorganised and given an independent commission—
" Crying down " of the currency—Erection of turn-
stiles in Bristol—" Certificate for eating of flesh in
Lent " granted to Corporation.*

THE sketch of corporate transactions down to the middle of
the sixteenth century, given in the three previous chapters,
has chiefly dealt with subjects relating to the internal
affairs of the city. Before proceeding further, a few
matters may be noticed in which the Common Council
were acted upon by outside influences. Feudal privileges,
for example, though decaying, were by no means extinct.
There were still many manors in Gloucestershire in which
the labouring population were serfs, attached to the soil
they cultivated, and liable to be transferred with the soil
from one owner to another. Many Bristolians living at
the accession of Henry VIII. must have remembered that,
less than thirty years previously Lord de la Warre, an
opulent local landowner, had threatened to recover as
one of his bondsmen a rich merchant, William Bird, who

had served the offices of Mayor and Sheriff of the town, his lordship claiming the right to treat the aged gentleman as a runaway beast, to take possession of his property, and to appropriate his family as " villeins." Happily Mr. Bird was able to prove beyond dispute that though his grandfather had lived for some years on one of De la Warre's manors, where his children were born, his ancestors had dwelt in Birmingham as free men for many genera- tions, and upon the Corporation taking action on behalf of a valued colleague, the peer found it prudent to abandon his claim.    The threat was, in fact, preposterous, it being one of the immemorial privileges of Bristol that a country- man who had lived for a year and a day within the walls was a townsman, and entitled to permanent protection. The issue was recorded in the Great Red Book at the Council House by a " Remembrance, to be had in perpetual memory for a president to all slanderous persons having their tongues more prompter to speak wickedly than to say truth."

Interference on the part of Royalty was a more serious matter.    Queen Anne Boleyn, during the brief period of her favour, followed the example of the courtiers around her, who habitually sold what influence they possessed to those willing to buy it.    In January, 1534, Her Majesty addressed what was practically a mandate to the Mayor and Corporation, requiring them to confer the next presentation of the Mastership of St. John's Hospital at Redcliff, of which they were patrons, upon two officers of her household and David Hutton, of Bristol, grocer, stating that they would appoint a fitting person when the office became vacant.    The Corporation obeyed the com- mand with great alacrity, the grant of the presentation to the Queen's nominees being made only four days after the date of her letter. Whether Mr. Hutton, who was doubtless the prompter of the transaction, got his money's worth for his money is a matter of conjecture. He was a man of good position, and had served the office of Sheriff. Probably, in consequence of this transaction, the Common Council passed an ordinance in 1551, forbidding any member suing the Crown for any office in the gift of the city on pain of being dismissed and disfranchised. Before dealing with the fate of the Hospital a further reference must be made to the Queen.

In 1535 the King paid a visit to Thornbury Castle, one of the fine estates of the Duke of Buckingham, whose judicial murder a few years earlier had been mainly determined upon and ruthlessly perpetrated for the sake of cutting off a nobleman whose royal descent was a standing menace whilst there was no male heir to the Crown, and whose vast possessions aroused the greed of an unscrupulous despot. Henry was accompanied by his second consort, and they purposed to pay a visit to Bristol, but had to abandon that project through a deadly outbreak of the plague. The Corporation manifested much anxiety to propitiate their formidable Sovereign. Ten fat oxen and forty sheep were forwarded to plenish the Royal larder, and Queen Anne was presented with a massive gilt cup, containing 100 marks in gold, as the offering of "The Queen's Chamber," the title proudly claimed for Bristol. The gay recipient then little imagined that she was within nine months of her doom.

Reverting to St. John's Hospital, it would appear that the mastership did not fall vacant until 1542, when one Bromefield, presumably Hutton's nominee, was appointed ; but the institution was suppressed and its estates confiscated in March, 1544. The Corporation immediately attempted to obtain a grant of the spoil.  A deputation was sent up to Court, and the Members of Parliament rendered earnest assistance.  The expenses of the Chamberlain during this negotiation appear in the audit book, and afford a striking illustration of the cheapness of travelling at that period.  The officer and his man were absent fifteen days, and the total outlay for their maintenance and that of their horses at inns on the road and in London was 38s. 8d., being less than 1s. 3½d. per day for each man and his horse.  The hire of two horses cost 11s., or 4½d. per horse per day.  The servant's wages were 5s., or 4d. per day, and a special breakfast for the city members " for their pains," at a London tavern, cost 4½d. per head.

The corporate efforts were fruitless, the King giving the Hospital and all its belongings to his physician, George Owen.  The worthy doctor, however, seems to have had some compunction in appropriating a charitable foundation, for in 1553 he granted the Corporation a ninety-nine years' lease of numerous houses in Bristol, and 130 acres of land at Chew Magna, formerly belonging to the Hospital in trust, to maintain ten additional inmates in Foster's Almshouses at a cost of about £15 a year.  At a later date the Corporation purchased the fee simple of this estate from Owen's representative, and in recent years the rents have brought in £1,500 a year to the Charity Trustees, one-sixth of the proceeds being credited to Foster's Almshouses and the remainder to the Grammar School.

One of the most vexatious and most lasting outside troubles of the Corporation was the claim of the Lord President of the Welsh Marches to contributions from Bristol towards the expenditure of his Council.  The courts of this great official were held at Gloucester, Ludlow, or Wigmore Castles, and it was his custom to assume that this city was within his jurisdiction, and to summon the Mayor to wait upon him and render military service and tribute for the defence of the Marches. The first recorded instance of this preposterous demand occurs in 1542, when the Chamberlain paid fees to two pursuivants bringing " commands " of this character, but no response seems to have been returned. In 1551 a similar mandate was issued by Sir William Herbert, Lord President, in a more peremptory style, and after vainly seeking protection in London, the civic body sent a deputation to Ludlow to protest against the aggression. The result must have been unsatisfactory, for further appeals were forthwith made by the Corporation to the Royal Court. A butt of wine, costing £8 10s., was ordered to be sent to " the Duke's grace of Somerset," and 33s. 4d. was paid for its carriage to London ; sugar loaves were forwarded to a judge and two legal officials, and directions were given to the city delegates to inquire " whether Sir Henry had any such authority to direct any such commission sent to the Mayor, or that we were within his Principality of the Marches, and how London was served in this case." The Lord Chancellor at length ordered the issue of a writ of oyer and terminer to settle the question, but there is no record of the result.

In 1558 renewed arbitrary injunctions of the President provoked the Corporation to vigorous resistance, and the Chamberlain was sent up to London with a " Supplication to Parliament." What was more to the purpose in those days, a butt of " muscadel of Candia " was presented to the Lord Treasurer, whose secretaries and porters and various other underlings were duly " gratified," and

£6 13s. was given to the Solicitor-General " for his counsel and friendship." The Chamberlain was thereby enabled to return in triumph, bearing letters of rebuke to the President, which—submissive courtesy being no longer indispensable—were sent to Ludlow by a groom. Only four years later, however, in 1562, the claim was raised again in all its former extravagance, much to the indignation of the civic body. On this occasion, after a fruitless effort by the Chamberlain, from whom the President extorted 30s. for " harness, pikes, and other monyshyon," the Mayor, John Pykes, and some of his brethren, went in some pomp to London, and spent money so freely, yet so judiciously, that, according to a minute in one of the Council House books, " the citizens were exempted from the Marches of Wales for ever, which before it was great trouble unto them." The Mayor seized this opportunity to sue Queen Elizabeth for a charter granting additional privileges to the Corporation, and this effort, for the time unsuccessful, doubtless added to the civic outlay, which, owing to a widespread scattering of gratifications, including a black satin robe for the Lord Chief Justice, exceeded £200. Even after this crushing defeat, the Welsh officials had the audacity in 1586 to again assume suzerainty over Bristol ; but a journey to Court of one of the legal advisers of the city, possibly aided by " gratuities," put a final end to the Lord President's pretensions.

In times of scarcity the Common Council was accustomed to make purchases of corn for distribution amongst the poor at cost price, and had sometimes to go far afield for supplies. In 1531 a quantity of wheat was bought in the upper valley of the Severn, and was being brought down in boats, when, on reaching Gloucester, it was seized by the Sheriffs by direction of the Mayor, who had it sold, and coolly retained the proceeds. The Bristol authorities thereupon appealed to the Court of Star Chamber, which forthwith ordered the Gloucester officials to deliver at Bristol within six weeks as much good wheat as they had appropriated, whilst the impudent Mayor was summoned to London to answer for his conduct, and he and his Sheriffs were mulcted in £6 13s. 4d. each, to be paid to the Corporation of Bristol.

The corporate audit books for the first three years of Mary's reign have disappeared, and we are consequently deprived of information respecting the attitude of the local authorities in reference to the religious reaction of the time. The expense of burning unhappy Protestants must have fallen upon the civic purse, but as the records are lost, it is impossible to determine the precise number of victims, on which the old calendar writers strangely disagree. If it be true, and it is probably only too true, that the officers who carried out the sentences, instead of taking dry faggots from the plentiful stores on the quays, bought green wood at Redland to increase the agony of the sufferers, let us hope that the Corporation were not responsible for this additional torture. The account book for 1557 shows that the King and Queen's players and those of the Earl of Oxford visited the city to offer diversions amidst the prevailing horrors, and that the former were paid 15s. and the latter 10s. for the entertainments. It also appears that the Corporation had revived the celebration of Spencer's Obit in accordance with the original trust ; but this may have been due to compulsion ; and the flight of two of the city ministers to escape persecution indicates that in Bristol, as in London, Protestant doctrines had taken a deep root.

The accession of Elizabeth, which put an end to the reign of terror, was hailed with rejoicings and bonfires, and still greater manifestations of joy took place at her coronation. " Paid as a reward to the parson and clerk to sing Te Deum, commanded by the Mayor, 2s.," indicates that the Corporation refused to attend Mass at the Cathedral. The civic body soon after appealed to their new Sovereign for a confirmation of the city charters, and after some demur the petition was complied with, the huge patent entailing an outlay of about £50 in fees at Court.

The Government seems to have speedily taken a new departure in reference to the armed forces of this and other cities. The annual muster of the trained bands had been previously a mere form. In 1561, after some rusty old armour had been put in order at the expense of the Chamber, twenty " gunners " were dressed in uniforms, provided with gunpowder, paid 6s. 8d. each as " conduct money," and ordered off to take part in the general muster of Gloucestershire. Four civic visits were paid to Lord Chandos, Lord Lieutenant, in the course of the year, and he was presented with four hogsheads of wine. The inclusion of the Bristol force in that of the county, however, was regarded as derogatory. The Chamberlain was despatched to London to plead the privileges of the city, and by liberal presents to the proper officials, including a butt of sack to the Earl of Pembroke, Lord High Steward of Bristol, the messenger succeeded in obtaining a pledge that the city should henceforth receive an independent commission. Thereupon, " 12 ells of sarsenet, red, blue and yellow "—the city colours—were bought in London for £3 5s. to make a grand " ensign " for the troopers, which was decorated with " two buttons of gold, and tassells to hang at the top," and two drums were purchased to give a martial tone to the music of the city waits. All preparations being completed, the next year's muster of the trained bands took place in the Marsh before the Mayor and Corporation, who dispensed £4 16s. 8d. in gratifications to the captains, ensign-bearer, and other officers. The force was strong, having regard to the population, for in 1570 the Chamberlain laid out more than £65 in purchasing " 8 score cassocks (with laced sleeves), and 8 score breeches, for 8 score soldiers." Iron corslets and hand guns—then just coming into vogue—for twenty men were also stored in the Guildhall. After this reorganisation the saturnalia of the Watch Nights became less popular ; and in 1572 the Corporation laid out a large sum for " harness," which probably meant fire-arms, as shooting matches were fixed to take place in the Marsh on Midsummer Day, St. Peter's Day and St. Bartholomew's Day.

One of the greatest difficulties of the early years of Elizabeth's reign was the debasement of the currency perpetrated by Henry VIII. and the base ministers of his successor. With a view to restoration, repeated " cryings down " of the value of current coin were made by proclamation. At the first of these operations, in 1559, the Chamberlain obtained only 61s. 6d. for eighty-eight shillings, and on coins professing to be worth £10 9s. 6d. he lost £3 9s. 10d., or one-third of the face value. " The worser sort " of shillings, says a local chronicler— and the worser sort invariably passed as wages to the poor—were cried down to 2½d., causing infinite distress. All " outlandish money," which from its superior intrinsic value had come largely into circulation, was next forbidden to pass current, and the city treasurer lost some money on the French crowns and pistolets and Flemish angelettes that he had on hand. The Queen finally prohibited the use of base coin, and issued pieces which, though far inferior in value to the currency of the Plantagenets, were an enormous improvement on that of her father and brother, and afforded incalculable relief to the whole community.

The town wall, which at this period extended from the Froom near Thunderbolt Street to the Avon at the Welsh Back, had long been of no practical value for the defence of the city, and the gate in it, called the Marsh Gate, was merely an obstacle to traffic. During a riot in 1561, arising, it is said, out of the baptising of a child, the doors of this gate were removed, and they were never restored. But some substitute being thought necessary, the Council ordered the erection of a " turnpike," also called a " whirligig," and really a turnstile. Another whirligig was about the same time placed near the upper end of Steep Street, and doubtless stood at the top of a precipitous footpath on the site of the modern Christmas Steps. (Christmas Street had not then entirely lost its original name of Knifesmiths Street, and how the singular transformation was brought about remains a mystery.) There was a third whirligig in Tower Lane under the gate still standing there. It is not surprising to find that the turnstiles required as frequent renovations as the stocks, which the Corporation maintained in all parts of the city for the punishment of rogues, and were constantly in need of repair. Having mentioned this quaint instrument of correction, which each of the thousands of manors in England was bound to maintain, and which was everywhere to be seen down to about the beginning of Victoria's reign, it may be added that the corporate accounts contain numberless items for renewing or mending the Ducking Stool for ducking vixenish women, three of whom are

recorded to have been " washed " in a single day, that
the pillory was always getting worn out, and that a new
ladder for the gallows was required at short intervals.    A
cage for frantic disturbers of the peace, and a den styled
" Little Ease," in Newgate, were amongst the other
amenities of those good old days.

Elizabeth's Privy Council were accustomed to issue
a yearly proclamation forbidding all persons, save invalids,
from eating butchers' meat during the season of Lent.
The Corporation, however, sought some further relief
from the restriction, for the Chamberlain paid a yearly
fee of one shilling to " the Lord Keeper's man for entering
a certificate for eating of flesh in Lent," and this proceeding
gave so much satisfaction that the fee was doubled, and
was paid for many years.    But the Common Council on
one occasion presumed rather too far in its evasion of the
Royal commands.    In consideration of the sum of £13,
to be paid by yearly instalments, a licence was granted
to a butcher, living in one of the parishes outside the walls,
to sell meat to all comers throughout the forty days' fast.
But in 1570, when the favoured trader had paid £8 6s. 8d.
of the money, either the Butchers' Company raised a
clamour against the violation of their statutes, or some
informer had acquainted the Privy Council of the contempt
and induced it to send down a reprimand, for the Common
Council hurriedly revoked the licence, and ordered the
repayment of the amount received, declaring that " it
was not lawful to sell flesh contrary to the butchers'
ordinances."    Though the Royal mandate for abstinence
continued to be issued for more than half a century afterwards, the rapid growth of Puritanism caused it to be
ever less regarded, and except amongst a sprinkling of
High Churchmen, it was finally treated with contempt.

# CHAPTER V.

*Thorne family and Bristol Grammar School; St. Bartholomew's Hospital acquired; scandalous behaviour of the Corporation—Establishment of separate custom house at Gloucester, to the dismay of Bristolians— Payment to Members of Parliament—Visit to the city of Duke of Norfolk—Reformation of Bristol measures— Dispute between Corporation and Admiralty—Crest bestowed upon city by Clarencieux, King-of-Arms; copy of charter granting this crest—Earl of Leicester appointed Lord High Steward; his indifference to Bristol interests; his visits to the city.*

A DEED of conveyance made to the Corporation in July, 1561, by a citizen named Nicholas Thorne, for the alleged benefit of the Bristol Grammar School, is worthy of some attention, especially as all the statements hitherto published respecting the foundation of that institution are more or less defective and inaccurate. Robert Thorne, the grandfather of the above Nicholas, was a prosperous local merchant in the reign of Henry VII., and is asserted to have been one of the chief promoters of the memorable enterprise in which John Cabot discovered Newfoundland and the American mainland in 1497. He, or his son Robert, served as Mayor of Bristol in 1514-5, but he eventually removed to London, where he died in 1519. There is no bequest towards founding a school in his will, but from a circumstance to be noted presently, he probably left some private directions to his family and executors. His eldest son, Robert, who was M.P. for Bristol in 1523,

41

had spent his early life in Spain, where he acquired great wealth, and in 1532, in conjunction with his brother Nicholas and his father's surviving executor, John Goderich, he determined to found a grammar school.

There was at that date a hospital, almshouse and church dedicated of St. Bartholomew, to which the beautiful Early English gateway near the bottom of Christmas Steps is now the only existing relic. The charity was founded by one of the Barons De la Warre, and the living representative of that family was then the patron ; but the yearly value of the endowment hardly maintained the master and brethren, the buildings were falling into decay, and De la Warre's embarrassed resources rendered him desirous of being relieved of the institution. So on January 31st, 1532, an important legal document was executed by his lordship, with the assent and co-operation of the master of the hospital. It recited that agreements had been entered into between them and Robert Thorne, by which the latter had undertaken, provided the hospital and its estates were conveyed in fee to himself, his brother, and the above executor, to convert the buildings within six years into a convenient house for a grammar school, to provide a schoolmaster and usher, and to found a yearly obit service in the hospital church, at which ten priests and six clerks should pray for the welfare of De la Warre and the souls of all his ancestors. It had been further stipulated that the existing almspeople should remain in the hospital for their lives, receiving fourpence each per week for food, and that a priest should be maintained to pray daily for his lordship until the school was opened. In consideration of which covenants, De la Warre and the master renounced all rights and titles to the building and its estates for ever.

No mention is made of any pecuniary payment, but it is certain that the peer owed money to Thorne. The above transaction was illegal until it had obtained the assent of the Crown, but a licence in mortmain was granted by Henry VIII. in the following March, with permission to convey the property to the Corporation, in trust for Thorne's "laudable purpose." Robert Thorne died a few months afterwards, but had previously appointed the first schoolmaster (the school being temporarily held in a large room over Froom Gate), and he bequeathed by will £300, and a debt due from De la Warre, towards the "making up" of the new institution, besides devising several hundred pounds for various charitable purposes in Bristol. By his death, followed soon after by the demise of Goderich, Nicholas Thorne, the brother (Mayor in 1544-5), became seized in fee of the Bartholomew estate, but although he survived for many years, he took no steps to convey the property to the Corporation. In his last will, however, dated in August, 1546, a few days before his death, he directed the transfer to be made by his executors at the cost of his estate, and bequeathed a legacy, with his books, maps, &c., to the school. His eldest son, a little boy, thus became legal owner of the hospital, and nothing could be done by the executors. On the death of the youth, still under age, in 1557, the property devolved upon his next brother, Nicholas.

The Corporation now thought it time to intervene, and in 1558 Nicholas covenanted with the two Members of Parliament for the city that he would, on "coming of age," convey the property to the Corporation, on condition of being granted for a term of years or for life such portions of the estate as he might select. Accordingly, in July, 1561—as stated at the beginning of this chapter—he granted the estate to the civic body in fee simple, for the alleged purpose of carrying out his father's and uncle's intentions. Although some Corporate money was spent on taking possession of the charity lands, the whole affair was a delusive farce, and the conduct of the Corporation, clearly due to a secret arrangement, was almost incredibly scandalous. Nicholas Thorne having influential friends at the Council House, where he afterwards became Chamberlain, the Common Council, in the following September, demised to him and to his " heirs for ever ' the entire hospital estate (the school buildings excepted), reserving a ground rent of £30. In consequence of this conveyance, the property at his death devolved upon one of his daughters, Ann Pykes, as absolute owner, and she speedily raised a large sum by granting leases for considerable periods. Some public-spirited citizens, indignant at the malversation, at length sued the Lord Chancellor for an inquiry, with the result that the grant of the Corporation was adjudged to be fraudulent. Much litigation followed, and Mrs. Pykes, who stuck tenaciously to the property, was in 1610 allowed to retain it, on covenanting to pay £41 6s. 8d. per annum. The Common Council had by that time become ashamed of the misdoings of their predecessors, and in 1617 the charity lands were recovered for the benefit of the Grammar School by a payment of £650 to the illegitimate possessors. The estate now produces about £700 per annum.

In 1565 the Common Council learnt with consternation that an effort was being made by the inhabitants of Gloucester, then a " creek " of Bristol, to procure an independent Custom House for that port. Petitions against a proposal regarded as highly injurious to local commerce were hurriedly despatched to London, the Lord

Treasurer's aid was besought with a "gratification," and the rejection of the project was temporarily secured. In 1576 the Members of Parliament for Gloucester introduced a Bill to carry out the desire of their constituents, but it was stoutly opposed by their Bristol colleagues, Serjeant Walsh, Recorder, and Philip Langley, and was ultimately thrown out. But in 1580, to local dismay, Queen Elizabeth, by letters patent, established a Custom House at Gloucester, and attached to it the other upper creeks of the Severn. Earnest protests against this arrangement were addressed by the Corporation to the Privy Council, who, in 1582, directed a Commission to sit at Berkeley to inquire into the merits of the case. To meet the outlay incurred on this and other matters, the Common Council took the unusual course of levying a rate upon the citizens, which produced £80. A great effort was thereupon made to induce the Government to change its policy, the Recorder of London and other counsel being employed to set forth the ancient privileges of Bristol. In a petition to the Privy Council—the arguments of which do not hang very well together—the Corporation maintained that the up-country creeks of the Severn from Berkeley to Worcester had belonged to this port for time out of mind, that the chiefest vent of the city, as well as its chiefest source of grain and victuals, was the course of the Severn as far as Shrewsbury, and that the shutting up of this vent and supply by granting a Custom House to Gloucester threatened the imminent ruin of Bristolians. Gloucester, it was contended, was a place of no merchandise or trade, and what was adventured there to sea was only corn and prohibited exports, laden in small barks belonging to farmers and the like, to the defrauding of the Queen's Customs. Moreover, these barks were forced to lade and discharge at Gatcombe, fifteen miles below Gloucester, and the depth of water there would not accommodate even 50-ton ships, except at high tides.   Yet " Irish barks had found a direct trade to Gloucester, and all to ship away corn, and so we lose the benefit of their commodities and the uttering of our own."   " The trade and shipping of Bristol is already so decayed by reason of the premises that they have done away, and must do away, with their great shipping, and have offered them to be sold to their great loss."   It is finally prayed that, in regard to this urgent distress, the port of Bristol be restored to its ancient status.   The appeal met with no response.

The reference to the Irish demand for corn made in this petition confirms much other evidence in the Corporate books, to the effect that the sister island was frequently unable to grow sufficient grain to provide food for its population.

It has been already stated that the Members of Parliament for Bristol were paid " wages " of two shillings a day each during their attendance at Westminster.   The amount of their stipend had remained unaltered for over two centuries, and was originally fixed by statute.   The reduced value of money having been recognised in 1567, when the travelling expenses of the Chamberlain, with his servant and two horses, had risen from 2s. 7d. per day, the sum paid twenty years earlier, to 6s., the Common Council raised the Members' stipend to 3s. 4d. per day each, and a further grant of £12 was made for the hire and keep of their horses.   The Session had lasted ninety-eight days. In the next Parliament, in 1571—which sat for sixty-three days—the " wages " were increased to 4s. per day, and as the Members had been obliged to make two journeys up and down, the allowance for horses was £18 12s.   No further change was made for many years. In the following century the " wages " were increased to 6s. 8d. per day, but the grant for horses was abolished after the introduction of coach travelling.

In April, 1568, while the Duke of Norfolk was sojourning at Bath in company with the Earl of Worcester, Lord Berkeley, and other noblemen, six hogsheads of wine were bought for presentation to him by the Corporation of Bristol, and four of them were sent on to him with an invitation to visit the city, which his Grace accepted. The preparations for his reception were so extensive that rumours of his ambitious desire to marry the unhappy Queen of Scots, widely regarded as presumptive heir to the English Throne, must have reached the civic body. The shooting butts in the Marsh underwent extensive repairs, the exterior of the Guildhall was renovated, workmen were employed day and night in decorating it within with gold and colours, and a large sum was spent upon the stained-glass windows of St. George's Chapel and the Tolzey. A small outlay on the latter building— " Paid for burnishing the beasts upon the Tolzey "—is now inexplicable. Strangely enough, the expense of the Duke's reception and entertainment does not appear in the accounts, and was probably defrayed by subscription or a small rate. According to the chroniclers, his Grace, during his brief stay, attended service at St. Mary Redcliff, and proceeded then to Temple Church to watch the swaying motion of the tower whilst a peal was rung upon the bells, then a local marvel. His visit seems to have given umbrage at Court, and some annalists allege that he departed abruptly for London by command of the Queen. He was executed for alleged treason in 1572.

In the Middle Ages almost every corporate town

followed its own caprices in regard to the size of measures. Even to the present day, I believe, the so-called hogshead of cider at Taunton is of vastly dissimilar size from the hogshead at Gloucester, and the " gill " of beer at Newcastle is actually half a pint. Some reformation of Bristol measures was begun by the Common Council in 1569. In the accounts for March appears : " Paid for making the gallon of brass greater, which was done by John Coleman, tinker, 3s. 4d." The Mayor's kalendar states that four years later " the Mayor caused a good reformation to be made for measures of barrels and kilderkins, which were made larger and of a bigger assize than they were before. And the old vessels repelled."

The Corporation was much excited in 1569 by the wreck of a vessel, stated in one entry to have occurred at Portishead Point, while in a later, and doubtless more correct, statement the disaster is said to have taken place on " the rocks called Plotneys in Kingroad." In either case, Lord Berkeley, as lord of the manor of Portbury, claimed the ship and cargo, and ordered two of his officers to sell them, which appears to have been done. The Corporation, on the other hand, maintained that the derelict vessel and its contents belonged to the city by virtue of the Admiralty privileges granted by Royal charter. The dispute resulted in a law suit, brought to a hearing at Somerset Assizes, held at Chard in 1572, when a verdict was given for the Corporation, who recovered £16 damages and costs from one of Lord Berkeley's agents, whilst the other was consigned to a debtor's prison in default of doing likewise. The civic outlay had much exceeded the receipts. Some of the items are curious. The leading counsel for the plaintiffs received a fee of 20s., and two juniors 10s. each. The Clerk of the Crown, " for his favour touching expedition," had a tip of 10s., and " a dinner to the jury after the verdict " cost 12s. 11d. The Corporation at this period held an Admiralty Court yearly, sometimes at Clevedon, but more often at Portishead. The court was not held in a house, but in an arbour constructed of tree branches, and a good deal of gunpowder was spent in firing salutes. The outlay did not usually exceed £3 or £4, but in 1570, when the above dispute was pending, the civic body flouted Lord Berkeley by holding a court at Clevedon, before the Mayor, some of the aldermen, and many burgesses, to the number of 100 horses, besides footmen and sailors, when the outlay was upwards of £27. In 1574, when the contest was over, the authorities contented themselves with giving a " drinking " to the jury, at the economical outlay of 13s. 6d.

When the Corporation resolved on flaunting a gay ensign at the muster of the trained bands, as already related, annoyance seems to have been felt that the city arms were destitute of an heraldic crest and supporters, in the fashion of London. Application was consequently made to the Herald's College, and in 1569 Clarencieux, King-of-Arms, granted by his letters patent the required decorations for the modest consideration of £7. All Bristolians are acquainted with the extraordinary crest which this grotesque official bestowed upon the city. Perhaps they may be glad to have his explanation of the emblem. The Chamberlain records that a new Common Seal was at once engraven by Giles Unyt, goldsmith, the outer sides of which displayed the two unicorns as supporters, and at the top was the crest," the signification* of which is as followeth : Forasmuch as to the good government of a city pertaineth wisdom and justice,

* Given presumably by the inventor.

5

therefore the arms issuing out of the clouds signifieth that
all good gifts come from above ; the balance signifieth
right judgment ; the serpent signifieth wisdom ; the
nature of the unicorn is that unto those that be virtuous
they will do homage.   The wreath about the helm is
gold and gules, which is the colour that was devised by
the King of Heralds.   The lower part of the seal hath no
addition, save the subscription.''   The new seal cost £4.

The charter granting the crest runs as follows :—

TO   ALL   AND   SINGULAR   AS   WELL
NOBLES  AND  GENTLEMEN  as others to whom
these  presents  shall  come  ROBERT  COOKE
esquire alias CLARENCIEUX, Principall Heraulte
and king of armes of the southe easte and weste
partes of this realme of England from the river of
trent southwardes sendi the humble comendacons
and greeting FORASMOCHAS aunciently from the
begining the valiaunt and vertuous actes of worthi
persons have ben comended to the worlde with
sondry monumets and remembrances of their good
deserts, emongst the which the chiefest and most
usuall hathe ben the bearing of signes in shildes
caled armes which are evident demonstracons of
prowes diversly distributed accordinge to the qualities
and deserts of the persons meretinge the same to the
end that suche as have done comendable service to
their prince or contry eyther in warre or peace may
both receave due honor in their lives and also derive
the same successively to their posteretie after them
and WHEREAS THIS CITIE OF BRISTOLL
hath of long time ben incorporate by the name of
mayor and comonalty as by the moste noble prince

of famouse memory KING EDWARD the third
and lately confirmed by the QUENES MAJESTIE
that now is by the name and names as is aforesaid
by virtue of which corporation and sithens the first
grant thereof there hathe ben auncient armes incident unto the said mayor and comonaltie that is
to saye gules on a mount vert issuant out of a castle
silver uppon wave a ship golde YET NOTWITH-
STANDING UPPON divers considerations they
have required me the said Clarencieux king of armes
to grant to their auncient armes a creste withe supportars due and lawfull to be borne WHEREUPON
CONSIDERING their worthines and knowenge their
request to be reasonable I have by vertue of my
office of Clarencieux kinge of armes confirmed given
and granted unto John Stone now Mayor John
Hipsley recorder, David Harris Willm Pepwell
Robert Sayer Roger Jones and Willm Lawe, Aldermen, Thomas Crickland and Richard Yonge sherives
Robert Halton chamberlayn and Richard Willimot
towneclarke and to their successors in life office this
Creaste and supportars hereafter followenge that is
to say uppon the heaulme on a wreathe golde and
gules issuant out of the clowdes two armes in saltour
charnew in the one hand a serpent vert in the other
a pair of balance gold supported with two unicornes
seant gold mayned horned clayed sables mantled gules
doubled silver as more playnely aperth depicted in
the margent TO HAVE and HOLD THE SAID
armes creaste and supportars to the said mayor and
comonalty and to their successors and they it to use
beare and shew for ever more without impediment
let or interuption of any person or persons.  In

Witness whereof I have subscribed my hande and
set hereunto the seale of my office the fower and
twentithe day of August in the yere of our Lorde
God  A thousand fiv hondrethe thre score and
nyne and in the eleventh yere of the reigne of our
sovereigne lady Elizabethe by the grace of God
Queue of England France and Irelande Defendor of
the Faithe et cet.

> " ROBERT COOKE *Alias* CLARENCIEUX,
>     " Roy D'armes.

The Earl of Pembroke, who was appointed Lord High
Steward of the city on the fall from power of the Duke of
Somerset in 1549, died in 1570.   His lordship does not
seem to have used much influence at Court on behalf of
the city, though, of course, he was appealed to in
emergencies, and civic presents to him rarely appear in
the accounts.   On his demise the vacant post was solicited
by Lord Chandos, Lord-Lieutenant of Gloucestershire,
and also by the late Lord Steward's son ; but the Common
Council, always solicitous to ingratiate themselves with a
prominent courtier, bestowed the office on Elizabeth's
" Sweet Robin," the Earl of Leicester, of dubious fame.
Lord Chandos was consoled with the gift of a butt of sack,
whilst the Chamberlain, on going up to London to present
the civic patent to Leicester, got the help of the Recorder
in endeavouring to " pacify my Lord of Pembroke."
  The new Lord Steward proved to be a costly ornament.
In 1571 eight hogsheads of wine were sent to " Killing-
worth " by way of a boat to Bewdley, at a cost of £30 ;
two hogsheads of sack were bought for him in London in
the following year, and four hogsheads were sent to
Warwickshire in 1576.   The Corporation were in the

meantime beseeching him to obtain a licence from the Crown to purchase the weekly wool and cattle market in St. Thomas's Street, then belonging to the parish, in which he succeeded ; but its further suits for leave to farm the Customs of the port and for the appointment of a Bishop of Bristol (the See was then held in conjunction with that of Gloucester) were of no avail. The Chamberlain made many journeys to London in pursuit of these objects, and had, as usual, to give repeated bribes to secretaries and underlings to get an audience with the favourite, and " to keep his lordship in mind " of the city's desires. On Easter Eve, 1587, Leicester, accompanied by his brother the Earl of Warwick, paid a visit to Bristol, where elaborate preparations had been made to do them honour. For five days previously a band of drummers and fifers paraded streets, summoning the citizens to muster in arms to the receive them, and a grand " skirmish " took place on their arrival amidst salutes of cannon. Alderman Kitchin's house in Small Street, had been prepared for their lodgings, no less than £5 was given for the services of an imported cook, and the total cost of their entertainment, during a two nights' sojourn, exceeded £100, exclusive of over £23 for the horse meat of their retinue, which must have numbered several hundreds. After their departure on Monday morning, six horse-loads of sugar, marmalade, figs, and raisons followed them to Bath as a further compliment, but failed to render Lord Leicester happy. His lordship's sleeping accommodation in the sister city seems to have presented a sorry contrast to the luxurious provision made in Bristol, and as an effectual remedy for the shortcoming, he coolly asked Alderman Kitchin, who had accompanied the presents, for a gift of the bed on which he had reposed. The civic audit book shows that

the obsequious Corporation more than responded to the
request, despatching an entirely new bed, but apparently
allowing Mr. Kitchin to provide the bedding—

" Paid to Mrs. Blande for a feather bed with a
cannapayne and curtains of green sail belonging unto
him [the bed] £4.   To two labourers for fetching it to
Mr. Kitchin's house 4d., which bedding with the
appurtenances was sent to Bath to my Lord of
Leicester to lye in, who desired to have one for his
Bath bed.   Paid to a foot post for bringing a letter
from Mr. Kitchin to Mr. Mayor concerning the same
1s."

As no expense was incurred for removing the bed to
Bath, it may be presumed that Leicester made certain of
his prize by sending some of his servants to take charge
of it.

# CHAPTER VI.

*Purchase of stone coal by the Corporation—Case of Coun-
cillor John Lacie—Struggle between Corporation and
Merchant Venturers' Society ; ends in the monopoly of
the latter being abolished—Establishment of Meal
Market—Purchase of Brandon Hill summit—Visit of
Queen Elizabeth to Bristol ; lavish preparations for her
reception and entertainment ; Newgate prisoners receive
royal pardon—Outbreak of plague in the city—Piracy
in the Avon ; fate of the malefactors—Visits of travelling players to Bristol—Arrival in the port of three
vessels under command of Martin Frobisher—Celebration of twentieth year of Elizabeth's reign—Renovation
of quay walls by means of tombstones.*

ALTHOUGH surrounded by extensive coal-fields, Bristolians
of all classes long preferred the use of wood as fuel,
timber being extremely cheap owing to the vast extent of
Kingswood and other neighbouring forests. The winter
of 1570, however, was exceptionally rigorous, and through
the difficulties of transit, caused by heavy snowstorms,
the dearth of wood occasioned extreme distress. The
Corporation consequently ordered in several hundred horse
loads of " stone coal, to the intent to bring down " prices ;
and though there was some loss on the transaction, great
relief was afforded to the poor. Charcoal was the only fuel
purchased for the Council House for upwards of a century
afterwards.

The Common Council in 1571 were called upon to consider the case of an impoverished member of the body, and

adopted a singular expedient for his relief.   The following
item occurs in the Chamberlain's receipts :—

> " Received of John Lacie, mercer, in part payment
> of £10 fine, for that he should continue a burgess, being
> dismissed of the Common Council until he may be here-
> after called to the Common Council again when he shall
> be of better ability, £5."

As the remainder of the fine was never paid, it may be
inferred that Mr. Lacie did not recover his position.

The first record of a violently-contested election of
Members of Parliament for the city occurs in the spring of
1571.   The question involved in the struggle was one of
deep interest to the trading classes generally.   In the last
previous Parliament, in 1566, the Society of Merchant
Venturers had succeeded in obtaining an Act forbidding
any citizen, excepting members of the society, or persons
who had served an apprenticeship of seven years to a
merchant, from trafficking in merchandise beyond the
seas, upon pain of forfeiture of all the goods so imported
or exported.   The monoply thus established excited great
discontent amongst a numerous body of tradesmen who
had been accustomed to make small foreign adventures,
as well as amongst the workmen employed by them ;  and,
what was still more significant, the Common Council,
which for centuries had been dominated by the mercantile
interest, revolted against it, and supported the agitation
of the burgesses.   No details in reference to the election
have been preserved except that the contest was violent
and protracted, but the return of the Recorder as one of
the Members clearly marked the defeat of the Merchants'
Society.   The Corporation followed up this success by
appealing to Lord Burghley for a repeal of the Act, declared

to be injurious to the trade of the city, and a Bill to that effect was read a first time at the fifth sitting of the House of Commons, passed through all its stages in both Houses in despite of a vigorous resistance, and received the Royal Assent. In consequence of the struggle, the Common Council appears to have been the scene of frequent virulent disputes. During the year ending Michaelmas, 1572, the following receipts occur in the audit book :—

|  | £ | s. | d. |
|---|---|---|---|
| " Received of Mr. Snyg, for calling Mr. John Jones knave in his ear .. .. .. .. | 0 | 13 | 4 |
| Received of Mr. Langley (M.P.), for saying to Mr. Saxie : You belie me.. .. .. | 0 | 20 | 0 |
| Received of Mr. Robt. Taylor, merchant, for abusing Mr. Thomas Colston with contumelious words .. .. .. .. .. | 0 | 6 | 8 |
| Received of Mr. Robt. Cable, for abusing Mr. Richard Cole . .. .. .. .. | 0 | 6 | 8 " |

Strange to say, no ancient copy of the Act restoring freedom of trade to Bristolians is to be found in the city, and not even the slightest allusion to the statute is made in any of the local chronicles, or in the histories of Barrett, Seyer, Evans, Pryce, and Nicholls. Only the title of the measure, " A Bill for Bristowe," is given in the " Statutes at Large." But it is, of course, duly registered in the Chancery Rolls. During the Stewart dynasty the Merchants' Society made many efforts to procure its repeal, and the Corporation, again submissive to mercantile influences, were generally zealous in supporting the would-be monopolists, but the costly exertions proved fruitless, and were finally abandoned in despair.

All the markets in the city were at this time held in one

or the other of the principal streets, but the inconvenience
of dealing in flour and meal in the open air during wet
weather induced the Common Council in 1572 to order the
construction of a special building for the sale of those
articles.    The site chosen was a piece of vacant ground,
entered through a " freestone gateway," in Wine Street.
Towards the expense of the building, which cost about
£250, the Vestry of Christ Church made a donation of £10,
and a further sum of over £30 was extracted from two
soapmakers.    The Bristol merchants had at this period
acquired a large trade in the Mediterranean, and olive oil
being largely imported by them, they had induced the
Corporation to pass an ordinance prohibiting the manu-
facture of soap made of tallow or fish oil.    Owing to the
costliness of the foreign material, the ordinance was
frequently evaded ; but Mr. William Yate, a soapmaker,
whose dwelling closely adjoined the new Meal Market,
having been detected in boiling tallow, was now fined
£13 6s. 8d. for his infraction of the edict, whilst another
manufacturer is alleged to have given £20 " of his goodwill "—an assertion of doubtful credibility, seeing that he
was fined £10 in the following year " for boiling trayne
oil."    The Meal Market was for many years set apart during
the annual great fair for the accommodation of the
numerous goldsmiths from London and elsewhere who
attended to exhibit their wares.    In the troubled times of
the following century it seems to have been converted into
a guard house for soldiery.    The fine " freestone gateway " referred to above still remained, and was well known
to every citizen until its removal in 1881.    The crown of
the arch bore the letter " W " and the device of a gate,
from which the surname Yate was derived.
    One Walker, " the miller of Brandon Hill," turns up in

the civic accounts for 1573, having paid a trifling fine for breaking into the city pound and rescuing his horse, contrary to law.   The wooden windmill which stood on the summit of the hill was then a new structure, having been erected by William Rede, Town Clerk, who had obtained a sixty years' lease of Brandon Hill from the Corporation in 1564, at a rent of £1 6s. 8d.   Only a few years later, in 1581, both the civic body and its lessee were thrown into consternation by the property being claimed on behalf of the Crown.   A discovery had in fact been made that a small plot of ground on the top of the hill had been given by Robert, Earl of Gloucester, to Tewkesbury Abbey, when he founded St. James's Priory, but had escaped appropriation on the suppression of the monastries, doubtless from its yielding no rent.   The men who wormed out these facts thereupon petitioned Queen Elizabeth for a grant of the ground as " concealed Crown land," and this having been conceded to them at a fee farm rent of 5s., they demanded the estate from the Corporation, who were forced to buy their interest for the sum of £30.   As there is a common tradition that the Queen granted Brandon Hill to the city as a place to dry clothes, it may be added that the hill, with the exception of the above plot, had belonged to the Corporation from time immemorial, and that the right of free passage over it by the public, and of user by washerwomen, was formally recognised in a corporate document of 1533, before Elizabeth was born.

The year 1574 was long memorable amongst Bristolians for the magnificent entertainment of Queen Elizabeth during her " progress " through the Western Counties.   A visit had been anticipated in the summer of 1570, but after the Corporation, in a panic at its neglect of the roads near Newgate, had laid out a large sum on

repairs, the Queen altered her route. The assurance of
her arrival four years later induced the Common Council
to make unprecedented exertions to gratify their pomp-
loving Sovereign. It was in the first place resolved to
raise funds by a general " collection " from the inhabitants, which was doubtless effected by a rateable assessment. The amount thus secured was £535 1s. 7d.,
obtained as follows :—

| | | | |
|---|---:|---:|---:|
| All Saints' Ward   ..  ..  ..  .. | £173 | 10 | 0 |
| Trinity Ward ..  ..  ..  ..  .. | 104 | 7 | 0 |
| Mary-le-port Ward ..  ..  ..  .. | 91 | 4 | 7 |
| St. Ewen's Ward   ..  ..  ..  .. | 94 | 17 | 8 |
| Redcliff Ward ..  ..  ..  ..  .. | 71 | 2 | 4 |

A further sum of £450 was borrowed from charity
funds, " to be repaid as speedily as convenient," and the
Dean and Chapter contributed £5. Thus supplied, the
authorities proceeded to paint and gild the High Cross,
Lawford's Gate, Newgate, and Froom Gate, to order fifty-
three lighter loads of sand for the purpose of levelling the
streets, to purchase nearly two tons of gunpowder, to
collect one hundred and thirty pieces of cannon, to enrol
four hundred infantry clothed in the city uniform, and to
make various other provisions for her Majesty's entertainment. The Queen arrived on August 14. After making
a preliminary halt at St. Lawrence's Hospital for the
purpose of changing her travelling dress for more gorgeous
apparel, her Majesty advanced to Lawford's Gate, where
she was received by the Mayor and Common Council,
whose mouthpiece, the Recorder, addressed her in the
extravagantly flattering terms in which she delighted, and
presented her with a splendid purse containing £100 in
gold. The gay procession then started, and after a brief

stop at the High Cross, where " some pleasant sights were showed," and another at the Grammar School in Christmas Street, where the boys' poetical orations were so lengthy that they were brusquely cut short, the Royal visitor reached the Great House on St. Augustine's Back, the newly-finished mansion of Mr. John Young, which had been prepared for her reception, her arrival being saluted by deafening peals of cannon and musketry. The Queen remained in the city a week, and those desirous of details respecting the amusements offered her, consisting mainly of sham fighting on land and water and tedious rhymed twaddle by a man named Churchyard, may be referred to Nichols's *Progresses* and other works. Her Majesty rewarded her host with the honour of knighthood. The Corporate outlay during the visit was £1,053 14s. 11d., of which amount £37 were demanded by Royal officers, including the " Yeoman of the Bottles," for their fees.

The visit of Queen Elizabeth to Bristol subsequently involved the Corporation in an expenditure that appears to have been much begrudged. It is probable that when the Recorder, who lived at Wellington, near Taunton, travelled hither to take part in the Queen's reception, advantage was taken of the opportunity to hold the annual gaol delivery. At all events, when Elizabeth arrived nine prisoners condemned to death were lying in Newgate, and on the Queen becoming acquainted with the fact she intimated her intention of pardoning them as a special act of grace. The Royal word, however, did not satisfy the requirements of the law, which could be met only by a formal instrument under the Great Seal, and the Lord Chancellor and his subordinates forthwith came down upon the Corporation for the customary fees, amounting to over £14. The disgusted civic body had no alternative but to pay the money, but partially recouped itself by appealing for the assistance of the parish churches, by which £8 13s. 4d. were brought in, while the Bishop of Gloucester, who held the See of Bristol in commendam, forwarded a personal donation of £2 13s. 4d., thus reducing the civic outlay to a trifling sum.

The year 1575 was marked by a terrible visitation of plague, which broke out immediately after the great fair in July and continued its ravages for six months. Contemporary annalists assert that the victims numbered upwards of 1,900, but the figures are probably much exaggerated. Four ex-Mayors, three of whom were Aldermen, were, however, carried off. The virulence of epidemics in Bristol, as in other old towns, was doubtless largely attributable to the unhealthy supply of water, chiefly drawn from wells in close proximity to the parochial burial grounds, most of which were in crowded localities limited in area, and reeking with putridity. The quay pipe was supplied from an abundant spring, the so-called Boiling Well at Ashley ; but a large portion of the long conduit was unprotected, and the Chamberlain was incessantly called upon to remove the obstructions in covered pipe, caused by the bodies of dead cats. Thus, in December, 1574, he enters :—

" Paid for taking three cats out of the key pipe, where one was two yards long, five days, 5s. 6d."

The pestilence caused on this occasion a general prostration of local trade, and the depression was seriously aggravated by unprecedented disasters at sea. In November, 1576, the Chamberlain was despatched to London with a " supplication " to the Queen, representing the decay of the city and the lamentable condition of its merchants, through the recent loss of eleven ships and five barks—no inconsiderable proportion of the entire shipping of the port, which, according to an official report drawn up by the Customs officers, numbered only forty-four vessels in 1572. The petition was presented by Lord Leicester, but the applicants met with no warmer consolation than that " the Queen was very sorry." The commerce of Bristol did not recover from these disasters for upwards of thirty years.

An audacious act of piracy was committed in the Avon in July, 1577, by a gang of sailors and ruffians, who took forcible possession of a small Dungarven vessel lying at Pill, robbed several other ships laden with goods for the fair, and eventually sailed off with their booty. How an alarm was raised does not appear, but the record states that the pirates were pursued by " Lord Leicester's Flebote "—whatever that may have been—with a crew of sixty armed men, and that the villains, dreading capture, landed at Start Point, when all but four managed to escape. Those apprehended were tried at the gaol delivery in September, when three were sentenced to death, and one, says the Chamberlain, was " saved by his book "—an expression perfectly intelligible to every reader eighty years ago, but now requiring explanation. In the Middle Ages the ordinary criminal courts could not pass sentence on a felon (traitors excepted) who claimed to be in Holy Orders, and who was amenable only to an ecclesiastical tribunal. And as practically everyone, except a priest, was then illiterate, it became an established point in legal practice that a prisoner was to be deemed a cleric if he were able to read a certain verse, vulgarly known as the " neck verse," in the Book of Psalms. The unreasoning conservatism of the legal profession has, perhaps, no better illustration than the fact that the above privilege, commonly known as " benefit of clergy," was not abolished until 1827, although long before that date nearly every description of felony had been exempted from the relief by successive Acts of Parliament, and a thief might be hanged for stealing twelvepence-farthing. It may be added that criminals known to be laymen were entitled to the benefit only once, and that, to secure their conviction for a second offence, they were seared on the thumb for the first with a red-hot iron. Only a few weeks before the trial of the above pirates there is the following item in the civic accounts :—

> " Paid a smith for making iron cuffs, set in the Guildhall behind the prisoners' bar, for the burning of persons in the hand, 2s. 6d."

To return to the three convicts, the Corporation, believing that seafaring malefactors needed an impressive warning, resolved on hanging and gibbeting the criminals on Canons' Marsh, at the junction of the Avon and Froom, and in view of every passing vessel, the bodies being suspended so low that they were immersed at every high tide. The carpenter's wages for making the gibbet were still only one shilling per day, and those of two apprentices 1s. 2d.

A civic payment made to a travelling dramatic company in October, 1577, is of some interest to students of Elizabethan literature, inasmuch as it mentions the name of the play then performed. The record also indicates, for the first time, that the entertainment took place in the evening :—

> " Paid my Lord of Leicester's players . . . and for links to give light in the evening. The play was called ' Myngo.' £1 2s."

The audit book of the following year shows that six bands of comedians visited the city. Lord Berkeley's players are stated to have performed " What Mischief Worketh in the Mind of Man " ; Mr. C. Howard's " The [illegible] Ethiopian " ; The Earl of Suffolk's " The Court of Comfort " ; and the Earl of Bath's " Quid pro quo." The players of the Earl of Derby and the Lord Chamberlain afterwards appeared on successive nights in one week, but the Chamberlain, then and afterwards, failed to note the pieces performed.

Some excitement was caused in October, 1577, by the arrival in the port of two vessels under the command of the famous Martin Frobisher. The ships, according to the chroniclers, had come direct from Cattaie or Cataya, after a fruitless endeavour to discover a passage to India and China by way of the Arctic Seas. They brought home, however, a large quantity of ore, esteemed to be " very rich and full of gold," and on information being sent to the Government, the Privy Council directed that the treasure should be lodged for safety in the Castle until some specimens had been analysed. The stone eventually proved worthless. Frobisher also brought three " savages," doubtless Esquimaux, clothed in deer skins, but all of them died within a month of their arrival.

The " Virgin Queen " entered upon the twentieth year of her reign on November 17th, 1577, and the event was celebrated in Bristol in a manner that manifested the loyalty and affection of the citizens. The members of the Corporation, robed in scarlet, repaired to the Cathedral to " hear the sermon "—a mode of attending service that became more and more in favour with the growth of Puritanism—and on returning from church five trumpeters from the " Cataya " ships were engaged to head the civic procession and fill the air with martial music.  In the evening a great bonfire blazed before the High Cross. The demonstration was thenceforth repeated annually, and was continued for many years after the Queen's death.

The quays of the city being at this period in urgent need of repair, a strange expedient for their cheap renovation was devised by the Common Council.  The first mention of the matter occurs in the audit book, November, 1577, as follows :—

" Paid the churchwardens of St. Stephen's for one tombstone for the Quay wall, 4s."

Immediately afterwards four large tombstones and five sledge-loads of smaller stones (head-stones ?) were extracted from St. Lawrence's Church, adjoining St. John's, and another large block was taken from a church not specified.  Soon afterwards a ponderous stone, requiring " two brace of horses " to drag it, was removed from St. Lawrence's Church, and many similar abstractions are noted subsequently.  The ruined Friaries were further drawn upon, and a massive monument out of the demolished Carmelite Church was contributed by Sir John Young, of the Great House.  No reference to these desecrations is made by the annalists, nor do they mention the closing of St. Lawrence's Church, of which the Corporation were the patrons.  The deed annexing the parish to that of St. John, dated in March, 1580, asserts that the income of the former was only £4 10s., which was insufficient to maintain a minister.  The church was converted into a warehouse.  Its burial ground in Christmas Street, is believed to be now covered by the premises recently built by Messrs. J. S. Fry and Sons.

# CHAPTER VII.

## *Bristol Farthing.*

THE story of the curious square Bristol farthings, issued in the reign of Queen Elizabeth, has scarcely been alluded to by the historians of the city, being apparently regarded as unworthy the dignity of their works. Those grave writers little imagined that the tokens they contemptuously ignored would be so highly prized in our time that some of the aforesaid histories have become of less value in the market than the despised farthings—a variation from original prices that is likely to widen rather than diminish. Under the altered circumstances, local readers will perhaps be glad to have further information on the subject from authentic sources.

Down to the period at which this narrative has arrived, and indeed to a much later date, the English Government issued no coins inferior in value to the silver penny—a somewhat remarkable fact when it is remembered that the purchasable power of the Elizabethan penny was fully equal to that of the fourpence of modern days. To supply an obvious want, about the year 1574 certain tradesmen in various towns began to issue farthing tokens of lead, tin, mixed metal, and even of leather, and trouble speedily arose out of the valueless character of the pieces, which often could not be traced to the persons that profited largely by circulating them. That the grievance spread to this city is proved by a minute of the Privy Council, dated November 17th, 1577, ordering a letter to be sent to the Recorder of Bristol, Mr. Hannam, then practising in the Courts at Westminster, informing him that " certain small coins of copper," of which samples were enclosed, had been " lately stamped " in the city, " and not only uttered and received from man to man for farthings, but also current for that value almost throughout the country thereabout." The Recorder was further directed to make diligent inquiry on the spot by whom the coins had been issued, and by what means they had become so widely prevalent, and to certify the result without respect of persons. Oddly enough, there is no further mention of the subject in the Privy Council minutes. But the lacking information is supplied in the corporate records, which preserve a letter from the Privy Council to the Mayor dated three weeks later, December 8th, showing that the Recorder had not only fulfilled his mission with great alacrity, but had already forwarded its results to the Government. The Recorder had reported that the tokens in circulation were of numerous varieties, and were " uttered by innholders, bakers, brewers, and other victuallers, who refused to receive them again because divers had been counterfeited ; for remedy whereof, and for the benefit of the poor, the learned council of the city had advised the use of a general stamp," meaning doubtless a stamp belonging exclusively to the Corporation, through whom he transmitted his report. The letter to the Mayor then proceeds :—" The Privy Council very well allow this, and commend the providence of the citizens, and notify its contentment that the use of these farthings shall continue, provided that the quantity do not exceed the value of £30, and that they may be made current only within the city."

A warrant sanctioning the above privileges was brought down by two corporate delegates, whose travelling expenses were largely swollen by the extortions of Government officials. (The Corporation rewarded the Recorder, " for his pains," with a large sugarloaf costing 18d. per lb., and a gallon of wine.) And no time was lost in stamping tokens, for on January 14th, 1578, the Chamberlain records :—

> " Received of Mr. Mayor in copper tokens the sum of £15, to be delivered to the commons of this city and to be current for farthing tokens . . . according to the warrant procured by Mr. Smythes and Mr. John Cole, £15."

It is probable that these pieces were struck in London, and the cost included in the delegates' expenses.

Two further parcels, raising the issue to the sum of £30 fixed by the warrant, were received in July and September, " and the stamp was delivered to Mr. Mayor again." These pieces were struck by Edward Evenet, a local goldsmith, who was paid £5 for the copper and stamping, leaving the Corporation a clear profit of £10.

No issue took place in 1579. But in April, 1580, Evenet struck £15 worth " by command of the Mayor, the Recorder, and the Aldermen, for that there was a great want of them in the town," and the quantity was doubled in September. Notwithstanding this copious issue, the demand seems to have exceeded the supply, for in the audit book of 1581 are the following entries :—

> " Received of E. Evenet in copper tokens, stamped by warrant of the Mayor, Aldermen, and Recorder, in pursuance of the warrant of the Privy Council, which doth extend to the stamping of £30 worth at a time, £30."
>
> " Paid Evenet for stamping, £10."

The audit book for 1582 is lost, but it is not improbable that the civic body took further advantage of its profitable privilege. We have proof that in 1583 Evenet received fresh orders, and coined 28,800 tokens, using on this occasion " a new mould," costing 6s. 8d. In 1584 the Chamberlain journeyed to London for, amongst other matter, obtaining a renewal of the coinage warrant ; but no further issues took place for some years. Seeing, indeed, that in the previous six years the number of tokens known to have been coined was nearly 120,000, and may have been over 140,000. there could have been no real lack of small change. But when the legal pieces ceased to appear, knaves hastened to supply their place. In March, 1587, a butcher named Christopher Gallwey, having been convicted of " counterfeiting the copper tokens of this city to the great hurt and hindrance of the commons," paid a fine of £5. But many other swindlers must have been at work, for in the following month, apparently at the command of the Government, the Corporation bought up no less than 12,600 false tokens. The treasurer's record is :—

" Paid by the Mayor and Aldermen's command-ment, with the consent of the whole Common Council, according to a proclamation, to divers persons as well of the city as of the country, for divers sorts of copper tokens received of them because they were counter-feited by divers evil disposed persons, and therefore they were not allowed in this city, £13 2s. 11d."

No further mention of tokens occurred until 1594, when the Privy Council informed the Mayor by letter that it had come to their knowledge that many Bristol tradesmen had illegally stamped farthing tokens in brass

and lead, and, after uttering, had refused to accept them
again, whereby grievous inconvenience was caused to the
poor. The magistrates were ordered to suppress such
proceedings, and to compel the fraudulent utterers to
change the tokens for current money. The Corporation
thereupon obtained a fresh warrant from the Government,
authorising the issue of £40 worth of farthings, and paid
£7 for the warrant and 3s. 4d. for a new stamp. The cost
of stamping, including the copper, was now reduced to
4s. in the pound, and, though the Chamberlain was
allowed another shilling in the pound for his trouble in
paying them away to traders and workmen, the tokens
yielded a profit of 15s. in the pound. Whether this
lucrative business was or was not continued in 1595 is
unknown, owing to the disappearance of the accounts ;
but it was resumed in 1597, when Thomas Wall, a Bristol
goldsmith, was ordered to stamp to the value of £13 10s.,
the cost amounting to one fourth of the value as before.
Those two issues produced an aggregate of 51,360
farthings to be added to the figures already given. In
1598 the authorities ordered the preparation of an
improved mould, but this was never used. In fact, the
civic rulers, in their pursuit of gain, had overshot the
demand, and temporarily lost almost as much as had been
brought in. In the autumn of 1598 the Chamberlain
records :

"Paid out, for to take in brass tokens, to Thomas
Wall in money, £33 16s. 6d."

The loss was, however, partially redeemed in subsequent
years by cautious reissues. The whole of the authorised
Elizabethan tokens were square in shape, and bore the
letters "C.B." on one side, and the arms of the city, very

rudely cut, on the other.   Although only three moulds are mentioned in the accounts, they seem to have been more numerous, for Mr. H. B. Bowles, who has given much attention to the subject, and possesses a unique collection of English tokens, has noted eight varieties, some of which have the city arms reversed, that is, with the ship sailing to the right, but these may have been forgeries.   Few things, indeed, were easier to rogues than to counterfeit work so clumsy, and the temptation to do so was great when a shilling's worth of copper produced twenty shillings' worth of tokens.

On the accession of James I., the Corporation petitioned for a renewal of the lapsed privilege, but the prayer met with no response, and, as nothing was done by the Government, privately-issued tokens, many of the basest character, naturally reappeared.   In 1609 the celebrated Sir Robert Cotton, in urging the Government to issue a national copper coinage, aserted that not less than 6,000 traders in various parts of England were then every year casting lead tokens, practically valueless, yet of the pretended aggregate value of about £30,000, " whereof nine-tenths " disappeared yearly to the profit of the utterers.   His recommendation was not adopted, but in 1613 Lord Harrington was granted for three years the sole right of coining farthings, " to avoid the great abuse of leaden tokens made by the city of Bristol and others," and private coining was thenceforth forbidden.   No local tokens struck in lead appeared to have been preserved.

# CHAPTER VIII

*The Avon obstructed by a wreck—Soldiers quartered in Bristol en route to Ireland ; expense incurred by the Corporation—" Street pitcher " appointed—Difficulties in postal communication—New charter granted to Bristol ; heavy expenses involved in obtaining the title " City " — Bristol Parliamentary representative appointed Speaker of the House of Commons.*

A SHIPPING disaster, which appears to have long obstructed the navigation of the Avon, occurred at Hungroad in March, 1579, when a large vessel called the *Lion*, laden with Spanish salt and oil, struck the rocks and immediately foundered in the river. The Corporation called on a number of ship captains to superintend the raising of the ship, but the measures they took were unavailing, and the civic body, in great alarm, sought the advice of the Privy Council, apparently without result. At length, in May, the hulk was weighed and brought to shore ; but it soon afterwards slipped back into the river, and the situation became even worse than before. In spite of heavy expenditure, the tidal way was blocked for upwards of a year, and was cleared in April, 1580, only by tearing the wreck to pieces.

During the Irish rebellions of this period, the city suffered severely from the frequent presence of large bodies of soldiers, sent down from London for embarkation, but often detained for weeks by contrary winds. The troops, impressed from the lowest classes, spent their time in debauchery and rioting, setting the civic authorities, who

were required to feed them, at defiance.   In August, 1579,
when six hundred ruffians were lying here, the Chamberlain
paid 8s. 9d. " for making and setting up a gibbet in High
Street, to terrify the rage of the soldiers, who were so
unruly both in fighting and killing." This grim menace
proved so effectual that it was repeated on two subsequent
occasions.   In December of the same year another body
of one thousand troops arrived, but was speedily got rid of.
But a fresh batch of five hundred came down in July, 1580,
and was unable to sail for six weeks, during which disorders
were of frequent occurrence, the insolence of the bravoes
often bringing them into collision with pugnacious Bristolians, in which they were sometimes soundly punished.

The unruly soldiery were not the only trouble of the
Corporation.   The Government, in forwarding the men,
required the city to provide them, not only with rations
and pay, but sometimes with " conduct money " when they
departed, and shipping had also to be hired for their transport.   In the first of the above cases, the outlay was £483,
in the second £443, and in the third £1,160 ;  and those
large sums cannot have been raised without extreme
difficulty.   The embarrassment was still greater in the year
ending Michaelmas, 1581, when, owing to King Philip of
Spain sending some forces to assist the Irish rebels, the
Government despatched great reinforcements by way of
Bristol, and the corporate expenditure on them was about
£4,000.   In order to recover the money laid out on each
contingent, the Chamberlain had to ride up to Court, and,
as it was never an easy matter to wring money from the
penurious Queen, the unfortunate gentleman had much to
endure in following her about to country residences, and
" gratifying " officials for their help in getting his accounts
passed.   The following illustrates his vexations :—

"September, 1580. Paid one of my Lord Treasurers secretaries for his pains in examining my account, for it was very much misliked of and evil taken by my Lord Treasurer, because the charge was so great, being £1,160 8s. 8¾d., so that two days was spent in trying of the said account, which, thanks to God, could not be faulted in one halfpenny, 10s."

How the poor Chamberlain, who had only a single attendant, managed to convey large sums of money safely from London to Bristol (on one occasion he brought down £2,500) is a mystery. But though he was frequently on the road, and each journey to and from London occupied three or four days, he never encountered a mishap.

The rebellion partially collapsed in 1583, when the Mayor and his brethren were regaled at the Tolzey with a sight of the head of the revolted Earl of Desmond, "pickled in a pipkin," and on its way to gratify the Court.

It is stated in a previous chapter* that the task of paving the streets was at this period laid upon the proprietors of frontages, who were severally required to repair one-half of the street as far as the gutter that ran down the centre. As each owner fulfilled his duty at his own time and in his own fashion, the general result must have left much to be desired, and in September, 1579, the Corporation initiated a reform. The audit book records :

"Paid the new pitcher of the streets as a reward on his making his abode here until he pitches all the streets in the way agreed upon by Mr. Mayor and the Aldermen, and will take not above 1½d. per yard, and do his work well, 20s."

Further items in subsequent years show that the new official was vigorously at work. Difficulties, however,

* *Vide ante,* page 26.

arose in localities where there were houses only on one
side of the thoroughfare.  Such was the case at Redcliff
Hill, and in May, 1583, the Chamberlain paid sixpence
" to a drummer to get company together to carry stones
to mend the highway " at that spot.  The summons was
effectual, for four months later the civic treasurer dis-
bursed 4d. for ale drank by the Mayor and his brethren at
Redcliff Church style, doubtless after an inspection of the
repairs.

The difficulty of communicating with persons at a
distance before the establishment of a post-office is illustrated by the following item :—

" 1580, August.  Paid to Savage, the foot post, to
go to Wellington with a letter to the Recorder touching
the holding of the Sessions, and if not there to go to
Wimborne Minster, where he has a house, where he
found him, and returned with a letter ; which post was
six days upon that journey in very foul weather, and
I paid him for his pains 13s. 4d."

About the close of 1580 the Corporation resolved upon
petitioning the Queen for a new charter, empowering them
to increase the aldermanic body from six to twelve.  The
matter was placed in the hands of the Recorder, who was
furnished with funds to " gratify " the courtiers whose help
was desirable ;  but one of his disbursements proved dis-
appointing.  One Dr. Wilson,* it appears, received £10
upon his undertaking to obtain the Queen's signature
approving of the scheme, but the money was no sooner
pocketed than the doctor departed from Court, and is
heard of no more.  Secretary Walsingham proved a more
trustworthy friend, but other influential persons wanted

* Secretary of State and Dean of York, although a layman.

gratifications, and the affair still hung fire.  Nearly six months after the Wilson collapse, when the Attorney-General was on a visit to Ashton Court, the Corporation sent him a seven-pint bottle of "hullock" wine and half a pound of sugar, desiring to "understand his pleasure" respecting the delayed patent, and remarking that Walsingham's secretary had twice sent information that the Queen had signed the warrant.  Mr. Attorney, moved perhaps by the present, but more by the hope of favours to come, promised that the great seal should be appended with all speed, and this was actually accomplished in July, 1581, after the civic body had incurred some further expense in getting Bristol styled a "city" instead of a "town."  The Recorder, on his arrival with the charter—for which he had laid out £53—was welcomed with a present of two gallons of wine (Muscadel of Candia), and another gallon was sent to the Attorney-General, with the promise of a more substantial reward.  Four hogsheads of wine, costing £16, were next forwarded to Secretary Walsingham in gratitude for his services, £10 were given to the secretary's secretary for keeping his master "in mind" of the subject, and £5 were paid to the Attorney-General's clerk "for his travail."  The Chamberlain noted that Mr. Attorney and the Recorder were still to be suitably recompensed, but the following year's audit book is missing.

To meet the above expenditure, the ancient ordinances dealing rigorously with "foreigners" — that is non-freemen—trading in the city were brought into operation, the obnoxious class being offered the alternative of paying fines for admission as burgesses, or of having their places of business "shut down."  Three dyers were mulcted in £10 each, and two musicians, whose mode of gaining a livelihood is shrouded in darkness, paid 53s. 4d. each.

Numerous others were dealt with, and the total receipts from the process were £67 11s.

In January, 1581, at the opening of the third Session of Elizabeth's fourth Parliament—originally convoked nine years previously — John Popham, the senior Member for Bristol, was appointed to fill the vacant office of Speaker. The proceedings were of a peculiar character. When Popham's election was suggested, the Commons were informed that he had been withdrawn from his Parliamentary duties by the Upper House, which claimed his presence there as Solicitor-General. Applications for his release from this service having been made to the Lords, he was permitted to return to his proper place. The Corporation of Bristol, much gratified by the honour bestowed on the city representative, presented him with a hogshead of claret. Popham, who had resigned the office of Recorder a few years before, afterwards became the Lord Chief Justice, whose acquisition of Littlecote, the home of " Will Dayrell," was long regarded with deep suspicion by the people of Wiltshire.

# CHAPTER IX.

*Perambulation of city boundaries—Great dearth of 1585;
relief measures of the Corporation—Military enthusiasm; inspection of Bristol trained bands by
Earl of Pembroke; his disregard of mayoral precedence—Death of John Carr, founder of Queen
Elizabeth's Hospital—News received in Bristol of
death of Queen of Scots—Richard Fletcher appointed
Bishop of Bristol—Extraordinary feudal claim made
by Lord Stafford against Richard Cole; indifference of
the Corporation—Alice Cole—Increase in stipend of
Town Clerk—Fines for relief from office of Mayor—
Present to Lord Leicester—Fatal conflict in Kingroad,
due to attempted infringement of Bristol's monopoly of
hides and skins trade.*

A PERAMBULATION of the city boundaries took place in
September, 1584. A breakfast for the Mayor and Sheriffs,
consisting of seven quarts of wine and two pennyworth of
cakes, was the first feature of the proceedings. After the
" Shire stones " had been all duly visited, an afternoon
" drinking " disposed of a gallon of " Mathera "—
mentioned for the first time, and costing fourpence per
pint. The only other charge was 1s. 4d., " paid to
labourers to make the ways open."

The audit book for 1585 has not been preserved, and
we are consequently deprived of precise information
respecting the distress caused by the remarkable dearth
of that year, during which wheat rose to the famine price
of 110s. per quarter. The Corporation. adopted vigorous

measures for the relief of the poor, importing 4,000 bushels
of rye from Dantzic, and more than 1,000 bushels of
English grain, all of which was retailed at about cost
price.   Country bakers were also encouraged to bring in
supplies of bread, and although there appears to have
been some rioting, order was generally maintained.   An
attempt to ship off a quantity of butter, consigned to
France, was promptly defeated by the Mayor, who proceeded with a body of officers to Hungroad, boarded the
vessel, and brought away the cargo, which was sold in the
market at 2½d. per pound, whilst the sailors who had
attempted to resist the seizure were fined for the offence,
and lodged in prison until they paid the money.   The
dearth continued in 1586, but the Government rejected
the Corporation's appeal for permission to import foreign
grain.

The strained relations of the Government with King
Philip of Spain, and the unquestionable design of that
monarch to attempt the conquest of England, led to an
outburst of military enthusiasm throughout the country
in the closing months of 1585.   In November the
Common Council ordered a new " ancient," or banner,
for the trained bands, which were mustered in College
Green, and in the following month all the able-bodied
inhabitants were summoned by drums and fifes (which
the Chamberlain sometimes called phifes, and sometimes
fifties) to attend a general muster at Addercliff, now
Redcliff Parade, " to choose their corporals."   These
gatherings were preliminary to a grand inspection in
March, 1586, by the Earl of Pembroke, who had been
appointed Lord-Lieutenant of Bristol and Somerset.   The
Earl, who arrived with a guard of thirty-two horsemen,
was received with many demonstrations of respect.   A

large body of citizens in arms were in waiting, and thirty-two cannon fired a salute, whilst he was welcomed by the authorities. The mansion of Alderman Kitchin, in Small Street, had been prepared for his reception, and every available delicacy was provided for his entertainment. A pavilion was also erected in the Marsh for his use during the inspection. Finally, before his departure on the following day, he was feasted at a magnificent breakfast, and an immense present of sugar and sweetmeats, including two costly boxes of "marmalette"—one decorated with the arms of the Queen, and the other with his own—was offered for his acceptance. His visit cost the Corporation nearly £100, but in despite of their hospitality and tokens of respect the Earl's pique at being refused the office of Lord High Steward appears to have been still unallayed, and his arrogance in ignoring the Mayor's right of precedence in the city, by taking the "upper hand" of his chief host, gave so much offence that it was represented to the Queen, who, according to a local annalist, rebuked him for his presumption, and "committed him to the Tower until he paid a fine for the offence." The trained bands were mustered again in July, when a "picture of a man" was set up in the Marsh for gun practice, and a third muster took place in September. The Corporation did not bear any grudge against Lord Pembroke for his discourtesy, as in the following year, when there were pirates in the Severn, they equipped an armed pinnace to convey a barge laden with his goods from Bristol to his residence at Cardiff. But about the same time, on an appeal from the civic body, the Government appointed the Mayor Deputy-Lieutenant for the city, thus avoiding future collisions.

John Carr, a Bristolian, whose name is ever held to be

in honour as the founder of Queen Elizabeth's Hospital, died in June, 1596, aged about 52 years. Mr. Carr was the elder son of Alderman William Carr, a prosperous merchant and Member of Parliament for the city from 1559 to 1567, who was himself a local benefactor. The alderman purchased in 1562, for £3,500, the reversion in fee of the manor of Congresbury and Wick St. Lawrence, comprising about 5,000 acres of land, subject to the life interest of a lady who survived him; but £2,000 of the consideration remained unpaid at his death, when the net yearly value of the estate was estimated by an audacious jury at only £54. (Although somewhat less than half the manor now belongs to the hospital, the annual receipts exceed £4,500.) John Carr, on coming into possession, paid off the remainder of the purchase money. He was already an extensive soapmaker, having works not only in Bristol, but at Bow, near London, and made a discovery in his business which brought him large returns. He refers to this subject in his will, executed in April, 1586, as follows : " Whereas I have committed in trust to my servant John Dinnye, the trade of white soapmaking, a thing by me found out, and put in use here in England," and goes on to specify the manner in which the secret was to be confided, first to his widow, who was to have the profits for ten years, and afterwards to his relative, Simon Aldworth. Carr, though living in Baldwin Street, probably spent much of his time at his factory near London, for he had evidently paid much attention to Christ's Hospital, then a new institution, and resolved on founding a school of a similar character. His will accordingly directed that, after the payment of a number of legacies, and the liquidation of certain mortgages and other debts, which he anticipated would occupy five years, his executors should transfer his estate in Somerset, and most of his house property in Bristol, to the Corporation, in trust to found " a hospital or place for bringing up poor children and orphans, being men children," born of indigent or decayed parents in Bristol or on his estates, the system of governing which was to be modelled upon that in operation at Christ's Hospital. The testator trusted that the Corporation would erect a suitable building for this hospital, of which he made them " patrons, guiders, and governors for ever." The validity of Mr. Carr's will was disputed by his younger brother, the owner of the Woodspring Priory estate, but he withdrew his opposition on payment of £1,000, and on being released of a debt of £666 due to his brother's estate.

The Corporation displayed great earnestness in carrying out Mr. Carr's intentions, and hurried forward the period he had fixed for establishing the school by the payment of legacies, &c. Having effected their purpose within four years of his death, they obtained a charter from Queen Elizabeth, which, after reciting that they had " bestowed some thousands of pounds for more quickly hastening " Carr's pious object, constituted the Mayor and Common Council a distinct incorporation for the perpetual government of the charity, and relieved them from the restrictions of the statutes of mortmain, under which Carr's bequest was invalid. The applicants had doubtless flattered the Queen by beseeching her to become the patron of the intended institution, for the charter further directs that it shall be for ever styled the Hospital of Queen Elizabeth. The Corporation next resolved on granting to the school, in perpetuity, the mansion of the suppressed Monastery of the Gaunts and the adjoining orchard. The school was opened in the summer of 1590, when twelve boys were admitted. In 1597, in consequence of a bequest by one Anthony Standbanck, of several houses in the city in trust for the hospital, the Corporation obtained an Act of Parliament confirming the Queen's charter, and legalising the acceptance of Standbanck's estate. The subsequent history of the Corporate dealings with the school have been published in the Annals of Bristol in the seventeenth, eighteenth, and nineteenth centuries.

The Christmas week of 1586 is marked by two sadly significant entries in the Chamberlain's accounts. The first reads :—

" Paid a pursuivant for bringing down the proclamation concerning the treason done by the Queen of Scots, which proclamation was proclaimed on St. Stephen's Day, 13s. 4d."

As no one in those days escaped death when charged with treason by the Government, the next item is still more significant :—

" Paid for wood for and making a bonfire at the High Cross, when the proclamation was made, 3s. 4d."

The unfortunate Queen was executed on February 8th, after being much tormented by adjurations to forswear her faith on the part of Richard Fletcher, the servile and stonyhearted Dean of Peterborough. This man was appointed Bishop of Bristol in 1590 for his services in this tragedy and on condition of his granting the estates of the see to courtiers, which he did so extensively that he left little to his successors. He is said to have died from an immoderate indulgence in tobacco.

The minutes of the Privy Council acquaint us with an

incident which must have occasioned an extraordinary sensation in Bristol, yet which the local chroniclers, whilst carefully noting many trivialities, chose to utterly ignore. It appears that in the spring of 1586, when the office of Mayor was held by Richard Cole, a wealthy and widely-esteemed merchant, allied by marriage with two notable city families, the Smyths and the Carrs, the lord of the manor of Thornbury, Lord Stafford, claimed a right to seize the person and property of the chief magistrate and of his brother Thomas, also a merchant, alleging that they were both " villeins appurtenant " to his manor, and that he was as free to deal with them as with his cattle. His lordship having threatened to use personal violence for attaining his ends, the brothers appealed for protection to the Government, and on June 19th the Privy Council addressed a letter to Stafford, ordering him to forbear from arresting or molesting them and from disturbing them in their trade, seeing that they were prepared to answer his claim in the law courts. It was added that the principal officer of such a place, and his brother, having been, both themselves and their ancestors, always reputed freemen, should not be so hardly dealt with upon any supposition, and Lord Stafford was commanded to proceed no further until he had acquainted the Privy Council with the grounds of his pretensions.

His lordship does not appear to have paid much regard to these instructions, for another letter was sent down to him in July, when the Goverment had been informed that he had used violence and threats towards two country-men, contending that they were his bondsmen, and he was again forbidden to resort to force until he had legally proved his alleged rights. The mandate seems to have been dealt with as contemptuously as was its forerunner.

Nearly a year later, May 7th, 1587, the Privy Council addressed him again, pointing out that although he had raised no action at law against the Coles, and had refused to answer their suit against him, yet he had again violently attempted to seize them, and that they had been consequently forced to forebear from following their business. Such conduct was a breach of the Queen's peace, and he was summoned to appear before the Council to justify his conduct.   It seems clear that he was still refractory, for on November 15th the Council ordered that the continued complaints of the Coles and the claim of their persecutors should be heard and determined on December 5th by the Lord Chancellor and two other judges.   As there is no further reference to the case, the arrogant peer was doubtless defeated.   The most amazing fact in reference to the subject is that the Corporation apparently made no effort to defend the privileges of the city.

Alderman Richard Cole died in 1599.  In his will, which disposed of very extensive property in Bristol and Somerset, he bequeathed £30 to repair the road to Gloucester, near Newport, "where I was born." His widow, Alice, sister of John Carr, founder of Queen Elizabeth's Hospital, was a large benefactor to local charities, and the funds bequeathed by her are still administered by trustees.

The Corporation, in December, 1586, increased the stipend of the Town Clerk from £4 to £10 per annum. This amount, however, inadequately indicates the real official income, which was largely derived from fees.

For some unexplained reason, the civic body at this period experienced considerable difficulty in finding a well-to-do member disposed to take the office of Mayor. In the audit book for 1585-6 are the following entries :—

" Received of Alderman Browne, together with 11 pieces of ordnance, in consideration of being exempted for ever from the office of Mayoralty, £20."

" Received of Thomas Colston for the same consideration, £20."

It is somewhat remarkable that by much the largest fine paid for similar redemption does not appear in the accounts. Two years later, when the Common Council made one of its numerous but always unsuccessful attempts to reap a profit out of the House of Correction by setting the inmates to work—proposing on this occasion that the prisoners should dye and dress cloth—a " stock " of £50 was advanced to the keeper, which the Chamberlain notes was " part of the money given by William Young, merchant, in Mr. Cole's year (1585-6), to be discharged for ever of the office of Mayor." Nothing more is recorded respecting the dyeing industry, and in 1597 the Chamberlain paid £4 " for an iron mill for the House of Correction," the purpose of which is not explained.

About the date of the execution of the Queen of Scots the city authorities were thrown into a panic. The Chamberlain records :—

" 1587, February.—Paid to sundry persons who carried precepts of hue and cry to sundry places when the report was given that London was fired, and that armour should be in readiness, 3s. 6d."

The alarming incident is not mentioned by the local chroniclers.

An illustration of the Earl of Leicester's cool methods of procedure occured in the same month. The Corporation paid £42 for three butts of sack, which were ordered to be sent to the Archbishop of Canterbury, Lord Treasurer

Burghley and Leicester, " in hope of the continuance of
their goodwill and favour to the city." As Lord Leicester
was about to visit Bath, the butt intended for him seems
to have been retained until his arrival. The two others
were forwarded to London by a wainsman at a cost of £4 ;
but on their reaching the capital a servant of Leicester,
by his direction, tapped one of the huge pieces and ab-
stracted between three and four gallons of wine, which
the troubled Chamberlain had to supply by purchase
before making the presentation. In addition to the above .
gifts, the Corporation shortly afterwards sent a piece of
plate to Sir James Croft, a member of the Privy Council,
who had presumably taken umbrage at being unrewarded ;
and it was also deemed prudent to forward a rug coverlet,
costing £2 10s., to the Lord Treasurer's private secretary,
to keep him also in a good humour.

An account by a contemporary annalist of a fatal
conflict at Kingroad in July, 1587, incidentally throws
some light upon a profitable traffic of Bristol merchants,
which developed largely in the following century. The
exportation oversea of hides and skins was then forbidden
by statute. Nevertheless, some prominent local merchants
had, by a judicious offer of ready money and by undertaking to surrender a share of their yearly profits, induced
the avaricious Queen to override the law of the land by
granting them a licence to export calf skins, a material
in much demand on the Continent for conversion into
slim shoe leather. Agents were accordingly employed in
South Wales and the adjoining counties to buy up the
skins, but it may be presumed that the prices given were
considered inadequate, and that the exclusive privilege
of the Bristolians was regarded as unjust. At all events,
one Edward Whitson, a tanner in the Forest of Dean, in

concert with his neighbours, loaded a large boat in the Wye, near Tintern, with calf skins, in the hope of smuggling the cargo on board a French ship lying in Kingroad. It is probable that this is by no means the first effort made to evade the licensees, and that they had employed spies to give information, for knowledge of Whitson's design had reached the city before the departure of his boat. Mr. Thomas James (afterwards M.P.) and some other merchants interested in the business thereupon resolved on capturing the cargo by main force, and having armed themselves for the purpose, went down in a pinnace to await the smugglers. The latter, clearly foreseeing a collision, were provided with pikes, bows and arrows, targets, and leather coats. According to the local chronicler, the Forest men were the first to commence hostilities, and having wounded one of the Bristol crew with an arrow, someone, believed to be Mr. James, retaliated by firing a musket, by which one Gitton, the owner of the other boat, was killed.

Nothing is said respecting the fate of the smuggled skins, and the subsequent proceedings are involved in some obscurity. A local annalist says that Mr. James was tried for manslaughter in the Admiralty Court in London, and as the Forest men (for conceivable reasons) did not attend to give evidence, he was acquitted. James must afterwards have appealed to the Government, for the Privy Council in the first place commanded his co-partners in the calf skin licence to pay a proportionate share of his expenses, which they had previously refused to do, and then (April, 1588) ordered the Mayor and Aldermen to summon the Sheriffs of Bristol of the previous year to make restitution of the money and goods that they had taken from James as a " composition " for

Gitton's death. The justices were further directed to require Christopher Whitson, a mercer, to give a bond in £1,000 for his appearance in the following term to answer charges that would be brought against him by the Crown. (James had probably alleged that Whitson had acted in collusion with his namesake in the Forest.) Notwithstanding this mandate, the Sheriffs refused to surrender the confiscated property, and the Privy Council had to content themselves with directing the Mayor to settle the dispute as he thought fit. But Whitson was arrested in November, 1588, and lodged in the Fleet Prison on no specified charge, and there he remained for upwards of two years. In December, 1590, he appealed for release to the Privy Council, who by that time had totally forgotten why he was apprehended. They now admitted that his case was " grievous," and asked the Lord Chief Baron for an explanation. His lordship replied that he knew nothing about the case, but that Whitson had been detained upon the " often and earnest motion " of Attorney-General Popham, doubtless a friend of James. Whitson afterwards became prosperous, and served the office of Mayor.

# CHAPTER X.

*Dispute between rector of St. Mary-le-port and his parishioners*
*—Spanish Armada : Bristol's contingent to national*
*fleet ; jubilation at rout of Spaniards—Trouble with*
*the Dutch ; William Colston—Lord Burghley created*
*Lord High Steward—Thrifty expenditure of the Cor-*
*poration—Purchase of coal for school over Froom Gate*
*—Relation of Corporation to orphans of city the subject*
*of a Parliamentary Bill (1597)—Arrival in Bristol of*
*Bishop Fletcher—Renovations and alterations of St.*
*Mark's Church—Depression of trade in Bristol—*
*Piratical exploits round British coast.*

QUEEN ELIZABETH, in November, 1587, appointed six
Commissioners to inquire into the merits of a singular
dispute between the Rev. A. Arthur, rector of St. Mary-
le-port, and his parishioners. The rector, on whose
petition the Commission was granted, had been appointed
to the living about eight years previously. He asserted
that the parishioners had for forty years concealed the fact
that the rectory was in the gift of the Crown, and had
appointed at their pleasure a mere " minister or curate,"
and appropriated the profits of the rectory. These profits
he claimed for the entire forty years. There is no record
of the Commissioners' decision, nor can any evidence be
discovered to support the allegation that the advowson
was the property of the Crown.

Though the sailing of the " Invincible Armada " of the
Spanish King had been postponed in 1587 through the
daring exploits of Drake and other causes, its approach in

the following year was regarded as certain, and the English people universally betook themselves to defensive preparations. In March the Bristolians were summoned to muster at Lady Day before their captain-general at Redcliff Church " to choose out trained soldiers," and a large force was soon in arms and regularly drilled. The Common Council ordered another new " ancient "—a gigantic banner composed of 37¾ yards of taffeta—and directed the portcullises at the city gates to be " looked unto," and the town walls to be repaired.

About the same time the Government, availing itself of the Royal prerogative under which shipmoney was claimed from maritime towns in case of emergency, demanded aid from every port in the shape of ships instead of coin. London was required to furnish eight ships fully manned, armed and provisioned. The call on Bristol, and also on Newcastle, was for three ships and a pinnace similarly provided. The outlay in these and minor incidents must have been raised by some form of local taxation on the inhabitants, but evidence on this point cannot be discovered.

This city's contingent to the national fleet—the *Great Unicorn*, the *Minion*, the *Handmaid*, and the *Aid*, provisioned for two months—sailed in April amidst enthusiastic farewells to join the Navy in the English Channel. The Government did not contribute a sixpence towards the expenditure, yet in June, when the victuals were exhausted, a letter was received from the Lord Admiral, requesting the city to furnish supplies. (Lord Howard was, in fact, unable to extract money from the Queen sufficient to victual her own ships.) The Corporation appealed to the Privy Council, representing that the citizens were utterly exhausted by the efforts already made, and were unable to bear any further charge ; but the Council insisted that the stores should be furnished without delay, promising to defray the outlay at a later date. The supplies were provided, but no repayment was ever received. At the great fair all the canvas offered for sale was bought up by order of the Government, and despatched to make tents for the vast army assembled at Tilbury.

The week was one of intense excitement, for the conflict was known to have begun ; and though the Queen's players came to town, and were rewarded with double the ordinary gift for their performance, the inhabitants were thinking of anything but the drama. The civic rulers sent off a messenger to the South Coast " to understand some news of the fleets," but the journey seems to have been fruitless. At length, early in August, a letter was received from London, bringing " certain news " of the ignominious flight of the Spaniards, when 13s. 4d. was paid to the bearer for his promptitude, and the city burst into jubilation, the Queen's " players and tumblers " adding an extra flash of gaiety to the rejoicings. The irritating old annalists do not afford a scrap of information as to the fate of the Bristol ships. No doubt, like nearly every crew in the fleet, the men had to take part in the final rout of the enemy when destitute of food and almost helpless from want of gunpowder, which no entreaties could induce Elizabeth to supply.

Whilst the country was threatened with the hostility of Philip II., the Government was frequently troubled by the animosity of the Dutch, who had been much exasperated by the Queen's tortuous policy during their long struggle for emancipation from Spanish tyranny. In February, 1588, the Privy Council addressed a letter to the Judge of the Admiralty Court, setting forth that upwards of a year previously William Colston, of Bristol, merchant (an ancestor direct or collateral of the great philanthropist), in satisfaction of spoils and wrongs inflicted on him by the Admiralty of Zealand, had seized a ship and cargo of a Zealander ; that the Privy Council, at the request of the Dutch Deputies, had given orders for the release of the vessel, on the undertaking of the Deputies that justice should be done to Colston ; that the latter, after labouring for ten months, had secured a judicial condemnation of the Zealand authorities ; and that nevertheless he could obtain no redress.  The Judge was therefore ordered to give directions for the seizure of any Zealand ship and cargo found in an English port—such ship to be detained for three months to give the Dutch Government an opportunity of complying with the judgment given against them.  If they neglected to do so, the ship and cargo were to be given up to Colston in satisfaction of his claims.  This order having proved of no effect, the Council, in the following May, sent fresh instructions to the Admiralty Judge, giving further particulars of Colston's grievances.  Their letter states that the Bristol ship was seized near Flushing in August, 1586, and confiscated, together with the cargo, the owner's loss being £2,286 ; and that, whilst Colston was on his way to seek relief, he was made prisoner by a Dunkirk rover, from whom he was forced to ransom himself, his total outlay being £600.  The interest on these losses amounted to £381, making his total claim against the States of Holland and Zealand £3,267. The Privy Council therefore orders the Judge to grant a commission for the arrest of Dutch ships until Colston obtained full satisfaction.  Being armed with this warrant, Mr. Colston thought himself entitled to follow the example set by the Dutch, and not merely recovered his claim, but continued to make further seizures. In August, however, he was peremptorily ordered by the Government to sell no more confiscated goods, and to appear before the Privy Council to render accounts. There is no further reference to the subject.

On the death, in September, 1588, of the Earl of Leicester—which Ben Jonson asserted was caused by a poisoned potion that the earl had prepared for his countess —the Common Council followed its usual course by conferring the High Stewardship of the city on Lord Burghley, the head of the Government. No opportunity was lost of conciliating the powerful minister. In 1590 his second son, William—afterwards Earl of Salisbury—visited Bristol, and was welcomed with a present of " 38 lbs. of sugar, two boxes of marmalade, gilded very fair, and four barrels of sucketts," entertainment being also provided for himself and retinue. In the following year a gift of an undescribed character, but costing £11 10s., was made to Burghley himself, who did not lose sight of his yearly " pension " of £4. A " sargeant Painter at Arms " was paid £3 for the Lord Treasurer's portrait, which was framed for 5s. and set up in the Council House, where it is still to be seen. In 1596 William Cecil, then become Secretary of State, was presented with a double gilt silver cup, weighing forty-four ounces, and costing £15 8s. The secretaries of both the ministers were duly and sometimes largely rewarded for keeping their masters " in mind " of the city's request. Gifts were, in fact, looked for by every important official. In 1594 a butt of sack was sent to another of the Queen's lovers, Lord Keeper Hatton, doubtless in return for some service. The Clerk of the Privy Council and the Clerk of the Crown also figure for handsome donations. In 1598 the Clerk of the Parliament

by some means got hold of two new white rugs, value
£5 4s., belonging to the Corporation, and "detained them,
in regard he had been our friend in the late Parliament."

Though sometimes over-reached in this way by high-
placed cormorants, the civic body was by no means
disposed to spend money profitlessly.   On one occasion,
when the Lord Admiral, according to the custom of his
predecessors, contested the city's right to hold an Admiralty Court, the Chamberlain bought a fine piece of plate
for him, in the hope that the gift would smooth over
difficulties, but finding his lordship intractable, the civic
agent gave the silversmith 10s. to refund the cast and take
the plate back again.

Fuel appears to have been at a very moderate price in
1589.   The Common Council having in that year established a school over Froom Gate, to teach children, not to
read, but "to knit worsted hosen," forty loads of stone
coal were purchased for 15s. to warm the large room.   At
the same time, six loads of charcoal and a double draught
of wood for the Tolzey fires cost 8s. 10d.   It is difficult to
determine the weight of a sledge load, but as butts of wine
containing nearly 120 gallons were certainly moved about
on sledges, a load of coal can hardly have been less than
one-third of a ton.   Firewood was cheap, owing to the
abundance of neighbouring timber.   Several trees were
cut down in Lewins Mead in 1589.

Information respecting an ancient Bristol custom,
established by a charter of Edward III. upwards of two
hundred years before this date, is furnished by the minutes
of the Privy Council in March, 1590.   In a letter to the
Mayor and his "assistants in Orphans' causes," their
lordships stated that they had been informed that the
chief magistrate of the city for the time being had always

been governor of orphans, and had provided for their education and the preservation of their estates in accordance with the city charters.  But the Council now understood that this good system was no longer carried out, and that orphans had been, and were likely to be, defrauded by persons having possession of their property, who refused to give the Mayor full information thereof. Their lordships, therefore, having regard for such orphans, command the Mayor and his brethren to pursue strictly the ancient practice ;  to summon all widows and guardians having the custody of orphans' money, goods or lands ; and to inquire whether any embezzlement had been attempted.  If such persons refused to produce a full account of the property committed to them, or resisted the Mayor's authority over the children, they were ordered to be imprisoned until they gave satisfaction.  It may be safely conjectured that the issue of this mandate had been privately solicited by the Corporation through some friend at Court at an earlier period.  Large sums bequeathed to children had frequently been brought into the city treasury, and remained there for several years until the infant owners attained full age, and whilst the Corporation in the meanwhile dealt with such funds at their discretion, there is no evidence that they rendered a fair interest on the capital.  The ancient custom consequently fell into disfavour, and testators sometimes gave specific directions to their executors to keep aloof from the orphans' court. The mandate of the Government having failed to effect its purpose, the Corporation, whilst promoting a Bill in Parliament in 1597 for confirming the establishment of Queen Elizabeth's Hospital, obtained the insertion of clauses empowering them to act as the Privy Council had directed, and authorising the Chamberlain to take possession of property when executors or trustees refused to give sureties for the faithful performance of their duties. It was, however, provided that if a testator limited the management of his estate to a parent, brother, or other relation of his children, or if such relation entered into sufficient bonds for securing the orphans' estates, the Mayor and his brethren were not to interfere. The decay of the old system thus continued, and it gradually became obsolete.

Dr. Fletcher, the supple divine in whose favour the See of Bristol was separated from that of Gloucester, after being practically extinct for forty-one years, made his appearance in the city in July, 1590, when he was welcomed by the Corporation, and presented with thirty gallons of sack and twenty pounds of sugar. From the wording of the Chamberlain's record of this gift, it is clear that the civic body were ignorant of even the name of the new prelate at his arrival. Being the Queen's Almoner and a sedulous courtier, the Bishop could spare little time for his episcopal duties ; but he made another brief visit two years later, when the Corporation, honouring the Almoner more than the cleric, gave him half a hundred-weight of sugar, which cost 1s. 1½d. per pound. In 1593 he was promoted to the See of Worcester, and the bishopric of Bristol, which he had greatly impoverished, remained vacant for ten years.

So far as can be discovered, the Corporation up to this time had never availed themselves of St. Mark's Church for religious purposes. The edifice was not, however, wholly deserted. Thomas Pinchin, one of the monks of the old Hospital (who were granted a yearly pension of £6 each when they were dispossessed of it by Henry VIII.), received £2 additional from the Corporation to act as Reader in the church, and resided in an adjoining tenement until his death, about forty-five years later, when a new " curate " was appointed, who also received 40s. yearly as " wages." On the establishment of Queen Elizabeth's Hospital, the Common Council seems to have resolved on alterations in the church with a view to accommodating the schoolboys. A stone pulpit was introduced, several old pews were removed to make way for benches, a number of new wainscot pews were constructed, and the entire interior was decorated plentifully with whitewash. The work went on day and night in order to be ready for the Queen's Accession Day, in November, 1590, from which one might presume that a civic visit in State was in contemplation; but if such had been purposed it was abandoned, for when the holiday arrived cushions were carried from the Tolzey to the Cathedral for the comfort of the worshipful body during the sermon. In the following March there is an interesting item in the Chamberlain's accounts, 10s. being paid to a mason " for removing the great tombs of the three founders of the Gaunts, which are now set at the upper end of the chancel." Their original position is, unfortunately, not recorded. Through corporate caprice at a later date, the tombs were removed to the south aisle of the church, where they still remain.

At this period the commerce of the city was in an extremely depressed state. The chief foreign trade of Bristol for several generations had been with Spain and Portugal, where vast quantities of fish, caught by local crews in the Northern Atlantic, were exchanged for the wines, fruit, and oil of the peninsula. This highly profitable traffic had been largely curtailed long before the outbreak of war by English adventurers like Drake, who, burning with indignation at the cruel persecution of the Protestants in the Netherlands, and at the tortures inflicted by the Spanish Inquisition on the crews of English ships carrying on an illicit traffic with King Philip's colonies in the New World, set international law at defiance, and took to the seas as systematic buccaneers. The eventual declaration of war between the two powers, of course, suspended legitimate trade altogether. Maritime relations with Southern France, the only other important centre of local commerce, were on an equally unsatisfactory footing, although the two Governments were ostensibly on friendly terms. The slaughter in 1572 of upwards of 50,000 Huguenots in France, commonly known as the massacre of St. Bartholomew, and hallowed by the exultant thanksgivings of the Pope, aroused a passionate thirst for vengeance throughout this country, and the bigotry of the infamous French King was met by a bigotry as remorseless as his own.

Happily, the many butcheries of Romish priests in England have no connection with local history. Elizabeth's efforts, or pretended efforts, to suppress filibustering on the ocean were powerless against the connivance of the whole sea-going population, of her own Customs officers, who claimed a share of the piratical spoils, and of the gentry and merchants of the West of England, who helped to equip the adventurers. One or two illustrations of the state into which legitimate commerce was brought under such circumstances may be offered from the State papers. In June, 1592, a French official, acting for the merchants of Bayonne, informed the Privy Council that in the previous year a ship belonging to that port was returning home with a cargo valued at 5,000 crowns, when she was captured by a vessel belonging to Sir Walter Raleigh, and taken to Uphill, near Weston-super-Mare, where certain rich merchants of Bristol received the cargo, and still held it, having forced the owner's agent to take to flight by threats against his life. In another case, reported by the same official, a still more valuable Bayonne ship and cargo had been captured by three English vessels, and taken into the port of Bristol, where several of the pirates lived, and the plunder was there openly sold, the ruined owner being refused redress. There is no evidence of any action having been taken against Raleigh and his accomplices.

The other affair was so discreditable to the second city in the kingdom that the Privy Council ordered the owners of the English ships to surrender half the cargo to the Bayonne man and to pay him £60—a sum so pitiful as to raise a suspicion that the Government sympathised with the freebooters. This mandate being coolly ignored, the Privy Council, after the lapse of another year, addressed a letter to the Mayor and Aldermen, desiring them to see that the Frenchman received satisfaction, and pointing out that further delay would provoke the French to equip privateers to prey on English commerce. The answer of the Corporation has perished. Whatever they may have done, the warning of the Privy Council was soon justified. In September, 1596, John Love and other Bristol merchants made a clamorous complaint to the Government that a French " piratical " vessel had seized their ship, the *Adventure*, whilst on her home voyage from Brest, laden with linen, canvas, &c., their total loss being estimated at £5,000. By that time the French had remonstrated against several other piratical acts of English rovers (one of which was partly owned by our old friend, Thomas James), and the Privy Council declined to take any action.

CHAPTER XI.

*Philip Langley fined in lieu of serving as Mayor—Further
attempt to deprive Bristol of its Admiralty jurisdiction
—Poverty of Bristol clergy—" Forlorn Hope " estate
of St. Nicholas—Court of the manor of Temple Fee
revived—Merchant Seamen's Almshouse founded—
Dealings of Corporation with John Whitson concerning purchase of corn—Ship-money revived ; in-
effectual protest of the Corporation—Repeal of " Re-
demptioner " ordinances—Piratical outrage of Captain
Thomas Webb—Claim of Corporation on Privy Council
for financial assistance—Bristol Fair—Visit to city
of Lord Essex, who becomes Lord High Steward ;
succeeded by Lord Treasurer Buckhurst.*

In February, 1592, Alderman Philip Langley was required by the Common Council to pay a fine of £50 for
being relieved for ever of the office of Mayor. The charge
seems to have been an unjust exaction, inasmuch as the
Alderman had served as chief magistrate ten years
previously. As he had also represented the city in
Parliament from 1571 to 1581, Mr. Langley was probably
far advanced in years.

The city audit books at this period are singularly
barren of interesting features. In 1592 the Lord Admiral
made another effort to deprive the Corporation of its
Admiralty jurisdiction, doubtless in order to secure the
fees and perquisites in maritime disputes and disasters
arising within the port ; and Dr. Julius Cæsar, Judge of
the Admiralty Court in London, was sent down as a special

Commissioner to investigate the subject. He held a prolonged inquiry, during which the civic body, which had already spent £30 in " gratifications " to courtiers in the hope of averting the attack, treated the learned visitor with profuse hospitality, and made him a costly present of sweetmeats. In the result, the chartered privileges of the city were found incontestable, and the Lord Admiral appears to have withdrawn his pretensions, though his defeat did not prevent some of his successors from asserting similar vexatious pretensions. The only other noticeable fact of the year was the capture of a porpoisé near Temple Back. It was presented to the Mayor for his personal delectation. The chief magistrate appears to have had peculiar rights over piscatory novelties. A few months later, on a " holibut " being discovered in the fish market, the Chamberlain bought it for 4s. and sent it to the Mayor, and in the following year his worship was the recipient of a sturgeon, caught in the Avon. The account books for 1593 and 1595 have perished.

An interesting letter, illustrating the impoverished condition of the Bristol clergy through the rapid spread of Puritanism, appears in the Privy Council minutes of March 16th, 1593. I have already drawn attention to the fact that the Corporation, when attending the Cathedral on State occasions, repaired there to hear, not the liturgy, but the " sermon." In this they followed the prevalent taste of the age ; and as many of the parochial incumbents, some of whom held other livings in the country, seem to have rarely preached, the yearly offerings that had once been voluntarily rendered to them by their city parishioners ceased to be given. The Privy Council, writing to the Mayor, Aldermen, and the Custos of the See of Bristol (then vacant), remark that they have been

informed that the state of the city clergy " is very mean
and poor," their benefices being for the most part not
worth more than £8 or £9 a year each, although in time
of superstition they yielded a sufficient maintenance for
learned men.   Their lordships had also been informed
that out of the common purse of the city a voluntary
contribution was made to maintain three " preachers,"
while wealthy citizens gave little or nothing to enlarge
the stipends of the poor incumbents.   The civic body
were therefore required to cause a reasonable assessment
to be imposed on such burgesses as did not contribute
towards the maintenance of the poor ministers, especially
of those who were preachers, and also towards supporting
common readers until by better encouragement the livings
might be furnished with able and learned men—a remark
far from complimentary to those actually in possession.
The names of persons refusing to subscribe were to be
sent up to the Council, with a report as to their means and
abilities.   The request of the Government was obeyed,
though the legal right of the Corporation to impose a tax
for such a purpose might well be questioned, and was
possibly repudiated by many citizens.   From a document
of a few years later date the annual sum raised was only
about £44, averaging less than £3 per parish.   Out of
this total the vicar of St. Nicholas, whose income was only
£2 13s. 4d., received £10, and the doles to his colleagues
varied from £6 to £1.   The " city preachers " maintained
by the Corporation appear to have received about £30
each per annum.

The value of the vicarage of St. Nicholas in 1428 was
officially reported to be £20, a sum certainly equivalent to
£50 in 1593.   During a period extending from about 1570
to 1593 the Vestry of St. Nicholas' parish received a number

of gifts and bequests from various citizens, who had directed that the yearly interest should be distributed amongst poor parishioners in doles of money or of bread. (It will be remembered that poor rates were still in the future.) The above benefactions appear to have been advanced in temporary loans on good security, with the ultimate view of making an advantageous purchase of land; and in March, 1594, when the fund at disposal amounted to £548, the Vestry, adding £42 to the total from the Church stock, acquired a house, garden, and about thirteen acres of meadow near Baptist Mills, in the parish of St. James, for £590. It may be assumed that from the outset the rent derived from the estate sufficed to produce the yearly gifts designed by the benefactors (about £30 in all), but it can scarcely have done more than this during the following century, owing to the purely rural character of the locality, and it is significant that the place obtained the name of the "Forlorn Hope." In course of time, however, the growth of the population in the district had its natural effect. A few houses were built on the property; the remainder of the meadow was divided into gardens, on which some occupiers "squatted" in wooden huts; and in 1821 the Vestry granted a new lease of the estate for seven years at a rental of £152. Until 1818 the parish authorities continued to pay the doles originally fixed by the donors of the charities, and made use of the surplus at their discretion. It was then determined, however, to apply all the proceeds (less one-fourteenth as the share of the Church stock) to the objects designed by the benefactor. This honourable conduct eventually plunged the Vestry into painful embarrassment. In 1857 the charity estates of the parish had risen in yearly value to £450, and the approaching termination of the lease of "Forlorn Hope" was expected to add £200 a year to that amount. Already, at every approach of the Christmas doles, the parish was inundated by worthless idlers and vagabonds, who hired a few nights' shelter to secure a share of the spoil, and spent their gains in vicious dissipation. The reform then effected is recorded in the *Annals of Bristol in the Nineteenth Century*. Since that date the old hovels on the " Forlorn Hope " estate have given place to several streets of substantial dwellings, which must have vastly increased the income of the charity.

In 1594 the Corporation revived the court of the manor of Temple Fee, so long held by the Knights of St. John. As the criminal jurisdiction of the court had been absorbed by the ordinary tribunals of the city, it is difficult to conjecture why the old institution was restored. It afforded, however, an opportunity for a feast, the Mayor and his brethren partaking of a dinner which cost £5. A separate banquet for the jurymen, who possibly presented " nuisances," entailed the modest outlay of 6s. 8d.

An entry in the minutes of the Privy Council, dated October 5th, 1595, affords information in reference to a still existing Bristol charity that was totally ignored by the old annalists, and is scarcely mentioned by many later historians. Very soon after the incorporation of the Merchant Venturers' Society by Edward VI. in December, 1552, this body acquired the desecrated Chapel of St. Clement (which had been built about half a century earlier by a fraternity of mariners), intending to use the building as their hall, and before October, 1561, they had erected, on an adjoining plot of ground, an almshouse for the for the reception of aged or impotent seamen. Most of the early records of the Society having perished, it is impossible to discover how arrangements were effected for maintaining this institution; but by some means the Merchants' Company were empowered to collect two small imposts to be presently described, and to extend their benevolent operations.  Addressing the Mayor and Aldermen on the date given above, the Privy Council state that they have been informed that in time past an almshouse was erected in Bristol for the relief of aged and infirm sailors, which was maintained by the levying of 1½d. per ton on goods, and one penny in the pound on sailors' wages, which imposts also supported a free school for sailors' children, and afforded a yearly stipend to a minister at Shirehampton Chapel for edifying the crews of the ships lying at Hungroad.  It being understood that this laudable and godly order was being withstood by some, especially by those going on fishing voyages to Newfoundland, to the impoverishment of the hospital, the Privy Council required the Mayor and Aldermen to assist the collectors in gathering the dues from those attempting to evade them.

The years from 1594 to 1597 were marked by disastrous harvests, and the distress amongst the poor of Bristol, great from the beginning of the dearth, increased to an appalling extent before its close.

A singular story concerning John Whitson's trading operations during this period is related in Adams' local chronicle, which states that the Mayor and Aldermen in November, 1595, foreseeing the probability of a great rise in the price of grain, commissioned Whitson to buy 3,000 quarters of Dantzic rye.  He consequently went to London and made a contract for that quantity at 28s. per quarter, to be delivered in the following May.  Subsequently the civic rulers repudiated the arrangement, declined to be responsible for more than half of the grain, throwing the risk of the other moiety on Whitson, and laid upon him

half the expense (over £8) incurred in making the bargain.
But when the cargoes arrived in July the prospect of
another bad harvest had raised the price of rye to 44s. per
quarter, showing an enormous profit on the adventure,
whereupon the worshipful Aldermen entreated Whitson·
to surrender his share of the gain, and offered him £50
for his trouble.    Adams goes on to say that Whitson,
being a good-natured man, consented to this cool pro-
position ; but the writer practically contradicts himself
on this point, for he adds that the Corporation, after a
gratis distribution of some pecks and half-bushels amongst
the poor, sold the bulk of the corn at 48s. per quarter,
and thereby cleared £774, whereas the profit must have·
been at least double that amount.    The Mayor's Kalendar
alleges that the corporate gain was £700, part of which
was expended in obtaining the Act for confirming the
customs of the Orphans' Court (already referred to).
That Act cannot have been very costly, and it is not a
little remarkable that not a trace of the funds derived
from this early exploit in municipal trading is to be found
in the civic accounts, with the exception of a payment of
£7 to Whitson for his charges for a journey to London to
buy rye for this city.    The foreign supplies, however, were
soon consumed, and in the closing months of the year
the scarcity amounted to an actual famine, one chronicler
recording that wheat rose for a time to the almost incredible price of 160s. per quarter.    The Privy Council
ordered the authorities of Gloucestershire and Worcester-
shire to permit corn to be sent down the Severn to Bristol
for the relief of the inhabitants, and similar mandates
were subsequently addressed to the justices of Wilts and
Somerset.    The Mayor's Kalendar states that the executors
of Robert Kitchin distributed £66 weekly out of his estate

amongst the suffering poor, but the most notable measure for relief was adopted by the Corporation, who ordered that the Mayor, the Aldermen, and every burgess " of any worth " should daily give, according to their respective means, one meal of meat to from two to eight destitute people, whereby all were saved from starving or rioting.

In February, 1596, Queen Elizabeth revived the unpopular impost of ship money, for the alleged purpose of defending the English Channel against the Spanish warships and Dunkirk privateers then ravaging English commerce. The demand made on Bristol was for three ships fully manned and provisioned, the outlay being estimated at £2,500. But of this sum Somerset was to contribute £600, the city of Gloucester (drawing £40 from Tewkesbury) £200, the city of Worcester £40, Shrewsbury £66, and Cardiff £40. In the mandate imposing the burden the Government ordered the Mayor and Aldermen not to extort more from those contributories than the sums specified. They were further directed to assemble all the able-bodied seamen in the port, and to impress as many of them as would be required to man the vessels.

These requirements extorted a wail from the Corporation, who, in a piteous supplication for relief addressed to the Privy Council, set forth the depressed condition of local commerce. The city, it was asserted, had become so poor that it was unable to bear the proposed burden. Londoners had not only monopolised its old and profitable trade with Southern Europe, but they had, through their riches, acquired the internal trade of the kingdom to within ten miles of Bristol, whose merchants could not gain by any possible adventure. Spanish commerce had once employed twenty or thirty tall ships here ; but King Philip's embargo and English reprisals had reduced this

fleet to eight or ten small vessels.  Such laden ships as now
entered the Avon mostly belonged to strangers, who would
not export Bristol goods, " whereby manufacturers are
towards an utter overthrow." The chief merchants of
the city, having lost hope, had retired from business and
retired into the country, whilst the meaner sort had spent
what they had, or were trading without advantage.
Londoners, in short, had monopolised everything.  " The
eagle followeth the carcase, and no wonder the enemy so
often falls upon them.   But that they, wealthy and strong,
should meanly press the Queen and our poor purses to
secure their own gains is surely a great wonder."   The
Privy Council, doubtless believing that these complaints
were exaggerated—although they unquestionably were
based on a sound substratum of truth—refused to abate
their demands.  Whereupon the Corporation, by levying
a rate upon the inhabitants, succeeded in meeting the
Queen's requirements, in despite of the Somerset gentry
withholding their quota, and the three ships fully equipped
joined the Royal Navy, and took part in the memorable
sack of Cadiz.   One of them was commanded by John
Hopkins, merchant, elected Mayor in 1600.

On their return, when the crews were paid off, the
Corporation made a fresh appeal to the Privy Council,
representing that Bristol merchants had lost £12,000 by
disasters at sea during the previous three years, and complaining that Somerset had obstinately evaded the
contribution imposed upon it.  The Government, ex-
pressing great satisfaction at the exertions of the citizens,
sent a strong remonstrance to the county authorities
against their unpatriotic lethargy, but the gentry still
sought to escape the charge by preserving a policy of
silence.   After a year's delay the Council sent down a

more imperative mandate, which produced nothing save a lamentation over agricultural distress, which was common to all parts of the kingdom. The Council next instructed Lord Chief Justice Popham to " persuade " the gentry to do their duty at the following assizes, and as Popham was presented soon afterwards with a butt of sack by the Corporation, it is probable that his remonstrances had a satisfactory result.

Some of the proceedings of the Common Council about this time were of a strangely reactionary character. During the early years of Elizabeth's reign the mediæval corporate laws debarring strangers from settling and carrying on trade in the city were so far relaxed that persons of that class were permitted to become freemen on the payment of moderate fines, and were known as " redemptioners." Though the reform must have tended to promote the general prosperity of the port, it was, of course, obnoxious to those selfishly animated by the old spirit of monopoly, and their jealousy seems at length to have permeated the civic body. On February 22nd, 1596, a corporate ordinance was passed absolutely forbidding any " foreign " merchant or trader to be admitted a burgess, either by redemption or on petition. An exception was made as regards artificers or men pursuing a manual occupation, but the qualifications of such applicants were to be carefully investigated by a special committee, the members of which were to be fined £100 if they contravened the true purpose of the ordinance. Even for mechanics the door of admission was rigidly guarded, for another ordinance of a few months previous date imposed a fine of 6s. 8d. per week upon every craftsman who employed a foreign or stranger workman bringing a wife or children into the city.

Some illustrations were given in a previous chapter of the piratical raids of English merchant ships against the commerce of foreign nations with whom the country was at peace.   Another local case of a revolting character is recorded in the Privy Council minutes dated June 24th, 1596.   In a warrant addressed to all the maritime officers of the Crown throughout the realm, the Council stated that they had been informed of a notable outrage committed by Thomas Webb, captain of the ship *Minion*, of Bristol [one of the Armada ships], upon a Dantzic vessel returning home with a cargo from Lisbon.   Webb had cruelly tortured the master and sailors, carried off the entire cargo, and despoiled the ship of her anchors and cables, whereby she was wrecked, and all on board were drowned. As the owners could obtain no redress, because Webb had sailed to Southampton and Bristol, where sundry of the inhabitants got possession of the plundered goods, and retained them under pretence of the Admiralty privileges of the two towns, the Crown officials were commanded to seize and sequester the merchandise, to stay the ship *Minion* for the better satisfaction of the aggrieved merchants, and to arrest and imprison Webb and his accomplices until they gave bail to stand their trial for the crime. Webb appears to have escaped, and his subordinates were long concealed through the connivance of sympathisers. In January, 1597, the Privy Council addressed a severe rebuke to the Mayor of Bristol, who, after the offenders had been arrested, had audaciously presumed to liberate three of them, although they were officers of the *Minion*, and Webb's chief instruments.   The Mayor was ordered to immediately recapture them, and to make them offer bail.   The record of the trial has unluckily perished.   It would be interesting to know whether Captain Webb was in any way connected with Alderman John Webb, who became Mayor of the city in the following September.

In the autumn of 1596, when the city was suffering under the terrible famine already noted,* the difficulties of the authorities were greatly increased by the arrival of large bodies of troops on their way to Ireland, who had to be lodged and fed whilst awaiting a favourable wind. The Government sought to alleviate the distress by directing the justices of Monmouth and Glamorganshire to facilitate the transport of grain from those counties to Bristol, but the relief can hardly have been important. The Corporation on this occasion claimed 8d. per day from the Privy Council for the diet of each soldier, and 10s. per head for their transport to the sister island, sums greatly in excess of the customary rates, and which led to an angry protest and demand for abatement on the part of the Council. The result does not appear. Having regard to the unprecedented price of bread, the charge for food does not seem excessive; but the passage money certainly appears exorbitant. Only eighteen months later the Chamberlain shipped off sixty-six Irish beggars to their own country at a cost of one shilling per head for the voyage.

The vast extent of business transacted at the celebrated Bristol fair is indicated by an entry in the Privy Council minutes for January, 1597. A large number of London tradesmen regularly attended the fair, bringing vast stocks of goods, and one of them, a mercer, sought the help of the Council at the above date, alleging that his servants, on returning home, were robbed of £1,700, besides bills and notes. At the fair in 1590 a party of Irish merchants brought such extensive cargoes of rugs and other material that they overstocked the market. Being unwilling to

* *Vide ante,* p. 107.

carry the goods back again, and the corporate laws forbidding strangers to open a shop, they made a bargain
with the Chamberlain, and paid a fine of £5 " for liberty to
sell to all foreigners for three days, after that the
citizens had first bought of them for three days before."
" Foreigners " were, of course, residents outside the city
boundaries.

The Virgin Queen's last favourite, the brilliant but
giddy-headed Earl of Essex, paid a visit to the city in
March, 1597, probably during a West-country tour.   His
lordship's position at Court being well known, preparations
were made for his reception, including the " cleansing of
the streets of filth " and decorating the High Cross ; and
a sumptuous entertainment awaited him at Mr. Haviland's
mansion in Small Street.   On January 13th, 1599, soon
after the death of Lord Burghley, the Corporation's invariable desire to secure a powerful friend in the Royal
Palace led to a hasty appointment that had to be regretted
at leisure.   The first entry in the earliest civic minute book
that has come down to us records the election at the above
date of the Earl of Essex, Earl Marshal, as High Steward
of Bristol " in as ample a manner as the office was hereto-
fore held."   A patent embellished with silk and gold
thereupon received the common seal, and the Chamberlain
was hurried off to London to present it to his lordship, and
to order a fine carving of the earl's arms for the decoration
of the Council House.   Before the ornament had been
received, the earl's star had begun to wane, through his
own wilfulness and incapacity, and a puerile seditious outbreak a few months later brought his head to the block on
Tower Hill.   Even before this catastrophe the Corporation recognised its blunder, and began its search for a more
stable patron.   It first besought the friendship of the

Queen's cousin and chamberlain, Lord Hunsdon, to whom a costly present of claret, " hullock," and sugar loaves was respectfully forwarded. Eventually, however, the civic rulers turned their devotions towards a more powerful minister, the Lord Treasurer Buckhurst, and tendered him a still larger token of homage.   On the execution of Essex, Buckhurst, of course, succeeded to the vacant High Stewardship.

# CHAPTER XII.

*Temporary policy of consideration by Government towards Bristol—Meat market established; friction between the Corporation and Bristol butchers—Cost of travelling in Elizabethan days—The " Great House" and Red Lodge—Assessment of the citizens—City roads repaired by compulsory co-operation of householders— Same method applied to maintenance of trained bands.*

THE heavy exactions on the city in the shape of ship-money, and the refusal of the Somerset gentry to contribute their quota of the impost, appear to have temporarily shamed the Government into a more liberal policy. Instead of extorting funds for feeding and shipping off troops for Ireland, as had been previously the invariable custom, remittances were sent down with the soldiers in 1597, and confided to the Corporation ; and on July 15th the Privy Council, in a letter to the Mayor, William Yate, greatly commended that gentleman's arrangements for victualling and transporting 800 men— a course of conduct, they added, that contrasted widely with the waste and private stealing that had been many times experienced at other ports. Such trust, so honourably discharged, continued the letter, moved the Council to think the Mayor meet to undertake further services, and he was therefore desired to buy up and transport victuals for the Irish army, which was clearly unable to find food in the devastated island. The customer of

Bristol had been ordered to advance money for carrying out these directions, and the justices of the neighbouring counties, including South Wales, were required to render the Mayor assistance in obtaining supplies. The considerate policy of the Court was of short duration. The next mention in the civic records of the migration of troops is a minute of a meeting of the Common Council, specially convened to demand loans from the members for feeding and transporting the men dumped down upon the city authorities.

Down to this period the meat market of the city was held in the open streets, and the setting up of stalls in the narrow thoroughfares must have greatly impeded locomotion. In 1598 the executors of Robert Kitchin, in accordance with the powers conferred upon them by the Alderman's will, devoted a portion of his estate to the erection of a covered market in the rear of a house on the east side of Broad Street, and transferred the building to the Corporation, who undertook to distribute the rents derived from standings in charitable benefactions. It would appear that the butchers were by no means desirous of being removed from their usual positions, and the Common Council, finding it prudent to respect ancient customs, were content to deal with the country tradesmen who brought in meat on market days, the " foreigners " being ordered, in April, 1599, to sell exclusively in the " New Market." Even this arrangement, however, was unsatisfactory to the resident purveyors, who speedily complained that their " stranger " rivals, instead of hastening to dispose of their goods and depart—as had been their previous habits—now compensated themselves for the tolls by loitering in their new quarters, to the great injury of local traders. Again bending to the free burgesses, the Council ordered, in the following June, that the countrymen should close their stalls at two o'clock in the winter months and an hour later in summer. The market was, nevertheless, still obnoxious to the Bristol butchers, and the civic rulers soon after appointed a committee to consider the desirability of closing the building altogether. The committee never produced a report, and there are indications that the selfishness of the complaining clique, who doubtless wished to establish a monopoly, brought about a corporate reaction. On December 4th, in consequence of an inordinate advance in the price of candles, the Council requested the Mayor and Aldermen to make an inquiry into the rates which the butchers were demanding for tallow, and to fix a reasonable price at which candles should be thenceforth sold. The butchers seem to have proved refractory, for the Common Council soon afterwards passed an Ordinance " to redress the excessive price of candles," giving chandlers in the neighbouring country districts full liberty to bring in and sell any quantity of candles, notwithstanding the ordinary laws against " foreign " commodities.

A concluding reference may be made to the cost of travelling in Elizabethan days. In the summer of 1599, after a review of the city-trained bands, the Chamberlain made a journey to Wilton to present the Muster Roll to the Earl of Pembroke, Lord Lieutenant, and not finding his lordship at home, followed him to Court. The worthy official was fifteen days on his travels, but his inn expenses and those of his manservant, including keep for two horses, amounted only to 6s. 8d. per day. The hire of two horses cost £2, and the servants' wages were 8d. a day. When in London the Chamberlain took the opportunity to

present the Clerk of the Privy Council, " for intelligence,"
with an Irish rug, purchased for £2. At this time a
swarm of Government officials received small pensions
from the Corporation, including the Clerk just referred
to, the Clerk of the Crown, the Clerk of the Exchequer,
and the Clerk of the Estreats—the last named con-
descending to accept 4s. 2d. a year, or about a penny
per week.

The story of the spoliation of the Bristol Friaries by
Henry VIII., narrated in the early part of this book, is re-
called to memory by an incident at this period that might
have furnished a new illustration to the celebrated Spelman
when inditing his denunciation of sacrilege. The Carmelite Friary, which stood on the site of the present Colston
Hall, together with a portion of its extensive gardens,
was acquired for an insignificant sum by the Corporation,
who soon afterwards sold the building and part of the
ground to Alderman Thomas Chester. The large upper
gardens, extending to what is now Park Row, fell into
the ever-greedy hands of Sir Ralph Sadleir, by whom
they were sold to a Bristol merchant named Rowland.
Early in the reign of Elizabeth a gentleman named John
Young, who had estates in Dorset and Wilts, determined
to settle in this city, where several of his ancestors had
been men of mark ; and having taken up his residence in
the above Friary, he resolved on constructing an imposing
mansion on the site. In February, 1568, he accordingly
purchased the old building from Alderman Chester, and
proceeded so vigorously with the erection of his " Great
House " that it served, in 1574, for the fitting reception
of Queen Elizabeth and her numerous suite during her
week's sojourn, during which its owner was knighted in
reward for his hospitality. Sir John was not satisfied

with this capacious residence. In 1578 he purchased from
the Corporation the remaining part of their estate,
consisting of a house and garden previously in the
occupation of Nicholas Thorne, and he at the same time
acquired Rowland's Lodge and garden on Stony Hill. On
this latter spot he forthwith set about the construction
of the large mansion now known as the Red Lodge, the
beautiful internal decoration of which remains to attest
his cultivated taste and ample means.

Sir John died in 1589, and it may be noted that at
the usual inquest held by the Crown to discover the extent
of his estates the jury declared on their oaths that the
yearly value of the Great House was 40s., and that of
the Red Lodge 20s. Their late owner left an only son,
Robert, then 19 years of age. Within seven years of his
attaining his majority, this young man appears to have
dissipated most of his fortune, and to have been over head
and ears in debt ; and on March 29th, 1599, being about
to adventure as a soldier in Ireland, and desirous of
protecting his Bristol estate from seizure by creditors, he
conveyed both the mansions to his half-brother, Nicholas
Strangeways, their mother's right to reside in the Great
House for life being reserved. Strangeways probably
disposed of the Red Lodge, but nothing more is recorded
about it in the Great Red Book at the Council House.
The prodigal returned from Ireland, where he obtained
the title of knight, but was probably poorer than ever.
Soon afterwards, in conjunction with Strangeways, he
sold the Great House for £660 to Sir Hugh Smyth, of
Long Ashton, and then vanished from history, nothing
being known of his ultimate fate. The Great House
subsequently became the residence and factory of two
notable sugar refiners—John Knight, followed by Richard

Lane, both of whom were Mayors of Bristol. The widow
of Lane conveyed the mansion, in 1708, for £1,300,
to Edward Colston, who there established his great
school.

Parliament having voted the Queen a subsidy in 1599,
a meeting of the Common Council was held in January,
1600, to assess the members of that body preliminary
to the collection of the impost. The proceedings, though
outwardly grave, were really of a farcical character. A
subsidy in boroughs was a tax of 2s. 8d. in the pound on
the value of each citizen's personal property, and in the
Middle Ages it was doubtless an onerous burden. But as
each community was assessed by Royal Commissioners
selected out of resident inhabitants, the gentlemen
chosen—with a tender respect for the pockets both of
themselves and their neighbours—gradually reduced the
charge by underestimating the value of the goods
assessed, and the results eventually assumed ludicrous
proportions. Thus on the above occasion, although
several members of the Council were merchants of great
wealth, with extensive stocks of merchandise, the maxi-
mum value of the property of any of them was alleged to
be £20, and only fourteen were stated to be worth that
amount, their less notable colleagues escaping with an
assessment of £10. The charge imposed on the general
mercantile and trading class is not recorded, but was
doubtless framed on a similar basis. It may be fairly
assumed that on the average the assessment did not
represent so much as one-twentieth of the actual property
of the taxpayers.

Having made this assessment, the Common Council
proceeded to make use of it for other purposes. The
roads leading into the city were generally in an execrable

condition, and in 1600 were so abominably bad as to force the Corporation to take action. On April 22nd it was accordingly resolved that every inhabitant " scassed " (assessed) in the subsidy book should pay after the rate of fourpence for every pound so scassed, and that this money should be employed in the reparation of the highways within the city liberties. It was further ordered that every householder free from the subsidy tax should work one day in the mending of the roads for the space of eight hours, bringing his own pickaxe and shovel at such time as he should be warned. Any person refusing to pay or to work was to incur a double penalty. This system of compulsory co-operation was in August applied towards maintaining the trained bands, wealthy citizens being required to pay the wages of one or more of the troopers summoned to the yearly muster, and to furnish each of such men with a coat, the penalty for disobeying the latter order being 20s. per man. Members of the Common Council were further required to provide arms and armour for the soldiers, and fifty corslets, forty-five guns, a few pikes, and twenty targets were forthwith brought in. The Corporation being in need of money, it was next resolved to raise £500 by loans for four years, the interest on which (probably eight or ten per cent.) was ordered to be defrayed by the members of the Council, who were to be taxed upon the basis of the subsidy book. Finally the old law was revived whereby a citizen was forbidden to sue a fellow burgess in any court save those of the mayor and sheriffs. A person who had presumed to raise an action of this kind in one of the courts at Westminster was fined £10, and on refusing to pay the penalty was " discommoned," and dealt with as a " foreigner."

A final extract, brief but interesting, may be made from the Chamberlain's accounts :—

1599, July. Paid for the sight of the model of Bristol, seen by Mr. Mayor and Aldermen, 5s.

What would the dignitaries of the twentieth century give to behold this remarkable picture of Bristol in the olden time ?

# INDEX.

1-month loans may be renewed by calling 642-3405
6-month loans may be recharged by bringing books to Circulation
Desk
Renewals and recharges may be made 4 days prior to due date

# DUE AS STAMPED BELOW

| | | |
|---|---|---|
| | | |
| | | |
| REC. CIR.    JUN    4    '79 | | |
| | | |
| | | |
| | | |
| | | |
| | | |
| | | |

Lightning Source UK Ltd.
Milton Keynes UK
UKHW02f1832260918
329588UK00019B/523/P